BLISS LAB

Bliss Lab

HOW THE ANCIENT YOGIS ACQUIRED
SUPERNORMAL POWERS AND HOW
YOU CAN TOO

Lalitha Donatella Riback

2019
GOLDEN DRAGONFLY PRESS

FIRST PRINT EDITION, January 2019
FIRST EBOOK EDITION, January 2019

ISBN–13: 978–1–7325772–6–8
ISBN–10: 1–7325772–6–9

Library of Congress Control Number: 2018967531

Printed on acid-free paper supplied by a Forest Stewardship Council-certified
provider. Cream paper is made from 30% post-consumer waste recycled material.

First published in the United States of America
by Golden Dragonfly Press, 2019.

www.shreemlab.com
www.goldendragonflypress.com

I dedicate *Bliss Lab* to Dr. Baskaran Pillai, Baba, who has been my spiritual teacher, inspiration and guiding light for many years.

CONTENTS

INTRODUCTION

Live the soul awareness—which is ananda. Ananda is bliss.

—DR. BASKARAN PILLAI

I f you're reading this, you have probably embraced the idea of self-development or personal development and want to uncover your purpose. Perhaps, you have a powerful longing for a life full of meaning, ease, abundance and beauty, and feel frustrated with the lack of a clear path that resonates with you. And you might feel that you have no time for joy, playfulness and contemplation. I've been there. At that time, I was eager to try anything that could be read, studied and compared, just so I could explore my spiritual self, and become a better version of myself.

Then I learned about the path of the ancient Rishis or intuitive seers and yogis of India, and traveled countless times to India, living there for over five years. Something about the incredible spiritual, scientific, emotional and intellectual intelligence within the Indian culture touched a chord in me so deeply that I was changed forever.

Fifteen years ago, when I read a book about the Siddhas, the most ancient lineage of spiritual scientists and healers, there was recognition in me, as if my soul had been waiting for eons and finally meeting with its destiny.

I've always had a great interest in humanity and the human spirit. As a child, I passionately read literature, as my journalist mother insisted I read the classics, and I was happy to do so. I began studying philosophy and psychology in my early teens.

Later, I curiously compared religions and different cultures, but something was missing—I was dissatisfied, and my desire for learning unstoppable. I wanted to know the world, how other populations lived and I wanted to speak their languages. Over all, I've studied 10 languages. I now realize I was simply interested in *consciousness*, though at the time I didn't know.

At that time, my connection with God was feeble, if not absent. And as a young adult, my compassion and unconditional love for every form of life that I'd felt as a child had become a pale memory. Yet I still didn't like hurting others, or gossip and didn't engage in such belittling conversations. I felt that veiled criticism was a form of abuse towards innocent and unaware individuals, and I felt their pain.

Sadly, I also felt a sense of separation, which most face on the earth plane. With peers, I was often disappointed due to my idealism, remembering small gestures of indifference or disloyalty for too long.

I never confronted anyone, though, and stayed friends—but slowly, I stopped trusting and speaking from the heart.

We all know how painful this separation feels, even when we're surrounded by many peers and family members.

Fortunately, my sensitivity grew in leaps and bounds—and this was a blessing in disguise, because how can we feel compassion for others' suffering if we become disconnected from our humanness and feelings? We would risk becoming robotic or desensitized, suppressing our emotions.

As an adult, it took me three decades of studies, travels and the sheer luck of meeting great spiritual masters to realize that there are spiritual solutions for nearly every problem. And that if you're so inclined, exploring your spiritual self, and identifying your purpose need not be difficult or slow.

Sharing My Experiences to Support Spiritual People

I wish that no one had to spend so many long years, taking endless detours, making mistakes that could easily be avoided with proper guidance.

And my mission is now to help and support those who have suffered from the stigma of feeling spiritual in this busy, overly secular world, yearning to know the Divine, and felt ridiculed or criticized by family members and peers, or received condescending looks from others. You are not alone!

I now believe that the spiritual work I've done so far can help you speed your healing process, and guide you to uncovering your gifts of intuition, personal power, and the immense creativity hidden in you. And it's a great honor for me to help you add more meaning and joy to your life, as you connect with your authentic, spiritual self.

You will see that when you connect and align yourself with your powerful spiritual nature, life becomes happier and more fulfilling.

This book is easy on beginners. I've explained various techniques and steps in simple language, and included only what worked for my family, friends, students, clients, and me.

Even if you've never practiced meditation or are not familiar with the Eastern wisdom traditions, in *Bliss Lab* you will find a friend who's been where you might be right now—thinking that life was mainly hard work and struggle, and craving peace and meaning. You will also find techniques that you can use to restore your joy of living and connection to all of life.

You'll see that when separation ends, there is a vast, loving space: the ever-connected cosmos of the ancient Rishis and yogis, who taught about our highest potential as a human race.

Their message is simple yet profound: *You are God and are infinitely powerful and loved.*

Yet if you are already an advanced meditator and spiritual seeker, this book's contents will add new layers to your knowledge and experience. I know that the results will be life changing, because of the amazing nature of these empowering, practical teachings that I will share with you.

Each spiritual law and real life stories will remind you that you can change and edit your life according to your dreams. And you deserve to live an abundant, happy, and satisfying life no matter what circumstances you're in right now.

How I Got Here

By age 25, my spiritual longing had vanished and was replaced by skepticism. And you might already know this: a life without God is no fun. Mine was all work and no joy. I wholeheartedly agree with Dr. Pillai, my spiritual teacher, when he says, *"The curse of the 21st century is a life without God."*

Of course, life tests our innocence, a quality often frowned upon in our society. So we put on a brave face, ask no questions, and begin working and producing. Living in a fragmented world that wants you to be 'street smart' and clever about the latest trends and technology takes time—and few can even find a moment to think of God.

There is education to get, work to do, then for most, marriage, children, and then aging—and we risk losing our energy and living a life that feels incomplete or worse, meaningless. Not that being married and having children isn't a perfect path—because it can be, so long as we're living our full potential as human beings.

I don't believe, however, that disenchantment begins in young adulthood. In fact, it often starts earlier, as goofy entertainment designed for children is increasingly filled with trivia, and plainly, tasteless language and ideas. Bathroom jokes abound and our children risk becoming desensitized at a young age.

There is also no fast solution to our current crisis of meaning. And I don't believe the solution can be found in watching viral videos about people falling from bikes, tripping in mud, or brushing their teeth in public for fun. If you work or search online, you know that this is literally true.

If you feel the pain from the current dumbing down of the global mind and want more love, happiness, spiritual fulfillment, and expressing your infinite potential—*Bliss Lab* is the book for you.

Is Vedic Astrology a Solution to Our Modern Problems?

Should you care about Vedic astrology? Fact: unlike other predictive systems, Vedic astrology comes equipped with many spiritual solutions. Soon you'll see the reasons why this system is called the Science of Light and is considered to be Divinely inspired. Moreover, Vedic astrology offers practical help to end suffering and solve relationship, financial and even health problems.

I've been interested in astrology since my teens, and a few years ago, I set out to write a book on miracles, yet it developed into this step-by-step guide to positive transformation with the help of Vedic astrology.

This is the system of the ancient seers of India, and I wanted to share with you some of its life-changing principles in clear, easy steps. In fact, I didn't want to write a technical book filled with complicated Sanskrit terms or rules of astronomical calculations, usually reserved for professional astrologers.

Other experts and authors have already written countless masterworks about this Vedic system, and these books alone require years and hard study to be fully explored. Here I want to mention my favorite Vedic astrologers of our modern times, K. N. Rao and the late Dr. B. V. Raman, and their priceless contributions to the world.

From the past, the two great Rishis *Bhrigu* and *Parashara* are my everyday guides—I literally pray to them before looking at birth charts and analyzing the influence of planets and constellations in my clients' lives. I have rarely found a discrepancy between the experiences of these individuals, their good fortunes and difficulties, and their planets' alignments. The rare times the planets didn't reflect the current life of that person was due to an incorrect time of birth. In fact, the planets are open books to astrologers: celestial bodies speak and you can speak to them.

Vedic astrologers are no ordinary people. They have the ability to talk and negotiate with planets.

—DR. PILLAI

Why Vedic?

Thousands of years ago, the world was blessed with the works of scientific, intellectual and spiritual geniuses: the enlightened and intuitive sages, yogis and astronomers of India.

Through long meditations, these sages had acquired extraordinary abilities, observing and accurately perceiving the cosmos, its laws and workings. Moreover, the seers were exceptional mathematicians who could count up to one trillion!

They called their astrological system *Jyotish* or Science of Light. Their noble goals were to become more conscious and illuminate the reasons behind birth and rebirth, the ups and downs of human life, and *karma* or the law of cause and effect. This system was designed only to help others and was used for one's self-development—so the Rishis or seers' reasons were pure and selfless.

Yet we can now enjoy the best of both worlds—as Vedic astrology can be used for practical applications to solve our everyday problems, and to make progress in our spiritual evolution.

Millionaires don't use astrology. Billionaires do.

—J.P. MORGAN

How does Vedic astrology work?

- It shines light onto the science of time
- Explains the law of causality, also known as the Law of Karma.
- It uses the principle of interconnectedness of all that is in the universe: *as above, so below.*

In ancient Vedic times, the Rishis realized the unique nature of time as a continuum of past, present and future—a concept that only recently has been explored by scientists.

The fact that the Rishis used a strictly scientific method was confirmed in 2004 by the Indian government and the Supreme Court of India, which declared Vedic astrology as accurate as computer science. Ever since, the *University Grants Commission* has been allowing students to earn degrees in Vedic astrology.

The Rishis had achieved higher states of consciousness and intuition—as a result of meditation. So no wonder they could predict the future and perfectly described our current era of confusion, the financial, spiritual and environmental crises, addictions, and the generally low morals seen in *Kali Yuga* or Era of Darkness. Many spiritual masters have announced that we're now reentering as a human race *Satya Yuga*, or the Era of Truth.

Why Bliss Lab?

The main inspiration behind this book is my immense passion for the healing sciences and spirituality, but also my great love for Vedic astrology, and its effectiveness in bringing happiness and positive transformation. As a professional astrologer and writer, I've helped thousands of people understand the reasons for their joys and challenges, and more importantly, how to end suffering to restore joy, hope, and find permanent solutions.

So *Bliss Lab* is for those beautiful souls who are tired of meaningless talks, uninspiring, dull activities, and soul-stifling work. Those amazing souls who aspire to relationship bliss, financial wealth, lasting well-being, and their unique life purpose.

If this is you, I have wonderful news—according to the great spiritual masters of India, life is meant to be an incredibly exciting and blissful experience. You will soon remember that you were born from a divine spark. Hence, you have all the glory of your divine inheritance deeply embedded in you.

I will guide you, step by step, to rediscover your inborn power of creation, which was known among the yogis as *thought manifestation.* You'll soon discover why you are made of light. You are meant to thrive and enjoy your life on earth.

Collectively it is our destiny to evolve to the next stage of human evolution. Those who want to make their mark on this planet and end the oppressive cycles of poverty, frustration, stress, fear, and boredom, will find support and value in *Bliss Lab.*

Thank you for taking this step and contributing with your spiritual unfolding to the evolution of this wonderful Planet!

My Promise to You

Do not identify yourself with your failures or your current state of frustration. This is the perfect time to plant the seed of your magnificent awakening and empowerment. And remember: your destiny can change in one second.

You have further support from the ascended masters, celestial archetypes, and seers, who have been guiding us like brilliant comets to our higher purpose and a life of bliss.

I promise that each chapter will come alive to guide you, transform you and help you make that small shift to a life of meaning and purpose. I also believe that the wonder, truth, and cosmic knowledge contained in the Science of Light are more relevant and useful as we now enter this new Era of Truth or Golden Age.

CHAPTER 1

How I Got to Vedic Astrology

I grew up in Italy. As soon as I learned to read, my greatest passions became books, archeology, mythology, and miracles. Yes—miracles. As young as six years old, I read and reread the same stories about Jesus and saints who performed miraculous feats. Of course, I also had a more common passion for dolls and toys.

According to Dr. Pillai, myths have a powerful impact on our consciousness. In fact, even when the rational mind struggles to understand the meaning of a myth, our subconscious minds make perfect sense of it.

In my case, mythology had a great role in my childhood, when I would enjoy reading epics of different cultures, and then daydream about the Gods of ancient times. I imagined what they would look like, and even tried to draw them on my design paper.

Schoolbook illustrations of pyramids, cities, mosaics, statues, silver and gold vessels from ancient sites made my heart soar with excitement. It seemed to me that the sculptures and paintings by the ancient people who depicted the Gods were evidence that these supernormal beings were real—and they definitely were for the populations of ancient Rome, Greece and Egypt—the main cultures studied in European schools.

Then at 18, I was given a book by the great Indian poet Tagore and I discovered India with its phantasmagoric, brightly sparkling colors and spiritual powers. What an impact those poems made on me! By comparison, my studies of Western literature, philosophy, psychology and languages had fizzled, and even made me depressed. I found that Tagore spoke to my heart, conveying so much beauty and spiritual depth that made me long for God and India.

Barely two years later, I was in Bombay and it was love at first sight. There I became acquainted with the Indian gods and goddesses—a multitude of celestial beings whose images peek at you from every corner, not only from the numerous temples.

After nearly three decades filled with the teachings of great spiritual masters, I've lost all doubts—for me the Gods of India are real, and I feel connected to them, the same as with Jesus, Mother Mary, saints, and angels. I've learned that these benevolent beings will communicate with you when you invoke them.

In India, I met my first Vedic astrologer and I was stunned.

You might have a trillion questions on how some star clusters and rocks can make or break your life. Despite their deceivingly inorganic appearance, the planets are alive and conscious, as the Rishis, or Vedic spiritual scientists, revealed thousands of years ago.

The planets' vibrations, rays, energy currents and magnetic fields influence the human body-mind and are a major source of both your thoughts and the experiences created by those thoughts. It might be difficult to imagine how something out there and far away like a celestial body can have an influence on our lives.

But one inkling of how these planets affect us can be found in the phenomenon of the tides or gravitational pull of the Moon that causes the rise and fall of sea levels. And it's well-known that our bodies are made primarily of water.

We can also look at the powerful effects a full Moon has on the human mind, a phenomenon that is well known in psychiatric hospitals. In fact, records show that the emotional effects of the full moon are so powerful that patients are found acting out more than usual.

Of course, the emotional states caused by the Moon are not always this dramatic. A full moon's strong effects can help you:

- Tap into your powerful emotions
- Visualize with unstoppable love and passion your heart's desire
- Manifest the fulfillment of your desires

The yogis knew that emotions are more powerful than thoughts.

Additionally, my teacher Dr. Pillai, who is an international thought leader, a scholar, spiritual master and mystic from India, has taught me that planets make our consciousness, and nothing happens on the earth plane without their influence.

I'm so grateful to have also studied Ayurveda and Vedanta from two other great teachers, medical doctors and experts of holistic medicine, Deepak Chopra and David Simon. In these studies, I learned amazing techniques for happiness, well-being, a meaningful life, and abundance.

Yogis and seers are tremendously conscious beings who created Vedic astrology.

—DR. PILLAI

Primarily, planets influence us through our thoughts—they act like powerful, magnetic fields that form consciousness and lead to perceptions, decisions and actions.

As another example, one can become a Bill Gates or a Steve Jobs thanks to planets that bring thoughts of wealth, prosperity and success. Vice versa, difficult planets bring negative thoughts that can lead to homelessness or sickness.

Of course, those are extreme cases of success and hardship—but I've learned that we're all born under the influence of planets, which deliver the fruits of our past actions or *karma*, the law of causality. Still, with the help of a skilled Vedic astrologer, stubbornly bad karma can be changed. And we can learn to think more beneficially.

It's important to say that we are not victims—we do have the capacity to remain alert and disallow destructive thought patterns. But without guidance, it is very difficult. Planets don't mean to harm us—they perform a very sacred duty by delivering the results of our thoughts and actions.

Although universal laws cannot be ignored—we can learn to understand them and work with them. You can even receive help, blessings and miracles, raise your consciousness, and perform good deeds—because nothing goes unnoticed—and good deeds are eventually rewarded.

While we cannot get away with any wrongdoing, as modern culture would sometimes have us believe, our lives can turn happier, more peaceful and meaningful as we align ourselves with the universal law of cause and effect.

> *Imagination is more important than knowledge. Knowledge is limited. Imagination encircles the world.*
>
> —ALBERT EINSTEIN

I spent nearly five years in South India, furthering my studies of yoga, Ayurveda, Vedic astrology and Vedic numerology, and traveling to magnificent hill towns, cities immersed in millennial beauty, and life-transforming spiritual sites.

Amazingly, there I saw indications of our incredible potential as a human race, and that we're all connected to each other and to a world of infinite possibilities.

Many secrets of our past and our immense potentiality can be found in the Vedas. Moreover, in beautiful India, you can merge with the consciousness of countless sages, and Tamil Siddhas, who are said to have amazing abilities of clairvoyance and other supernormal powers.

Both in the sprawling hills of Andhra Pradesh and the mounts of the Himalaya, I found many enchanting temples, some so tiny that you had to be taken there to find them. Whether they were Hindu or Buddhist, these places radiated Godliness.

But in Tamil Nadu, I was stunned by the powerful energy vortexes surrounding ancient temples that were off the tourist charts. These places of worship are believed to change the consciousness of its dwellers. And I was lucky to visit many such places with my teacher Dr. Pillai.

The Tamarind Tree and Other Mysteries

One night, Dr. Pillai took me along with a group of other students to a sacred temple in Tamil Nadu, his native state. In the surrounding garden, a tamarind tree stood majestic. Its leaves never closed up, remaining open even at night, unlike other tamarind trees. Both the temple and the tree were said to be thousands of years old. I checked on the leaves to prove to myself that they were really open. They were—and in the moonlight, they looked like thousands of tiny green fans.

Dr. Pillai told us that a great Siddha master had meditated there for many years in ancient times. We stood under the tree. "Place your hand on the tree," Dr. Pillai said.

As I placed my hand on the trunk, I watched the full moon peeking through the branches and the stars looking brighter away from city lights. Everyone stood silently with their hands on the tree.

Suddenly, I felt a swishing sound at the top of my head—as if my consciousness were leaving my body. I'd never had an out of body experience, and this sensation was totally new. 'Bliss' seemed like the most apt word to describe how I felt.

In another temple dedicated to Shiva, my heart and chest expanded so much that despite feeling fully alert and incredibly blissful, I couldn't put any words into my mind. That experience was likely what the Siddha Patanjali called *yoga*: "The cessation of the mind's fluctuations" or stopping the mind.

Once I had a Nadi or palm leaves reading. The astrologer didn't know anything about me—all he had was my thumbprint. Within a few minutes, he told me my parents' names, my grandparents' names, exact episodes from my childhood and youth that no one else could have known. He also described my problems, all with extreme accuracy. He added that my challenges were due to a previous life I had lived, in which I had accumulated a certain type of karma. His description of that life rang real to my ears—it fit my taste and childhood play when I insisted to dress up in beautiful clothes in the elegant, feminine style of a certain historic period. I would have my sister dress up the same way.

My remedies prescribed by the astrologer to fix me consisted in visiting certain temple vortexes to change my consciousness and receive miracles. As it turned out, these remedies brought me relief and lasting solutions in a short period of time!

Now I can understand why even Steve Jobs and Mark Zuckerberg went to India to visit Kainchi Dham Ashram in Nainital in Uttarakhand. This ashram belonged to Neem Karoli Baba, Steve Jobs' spiritual teacher. At the time Zuckerberg visited, he was facing an impasse with Facebook. Recalling the episode in an interview, he said that visiting that hermitage was critical for his later development and success of Facebook.

To other countries, I may go as a tourist, but to India, I come as a pilgrim.

—MARTIN LUTHER KING, JR.

Heritage from the Rishis and Siddhas

Guru is one who knows God, and who shows the way to Him. To follow a divine manifestation is the sure way to God realization.

—PARAMAHANSA YOGANANDA

Throughout millennia, Rishis and Siddhas worked tirelessly to help humanity evolve. When you learn how to tap into their extraordinary wisdom and use their tools for happiness and evolution, your life takes on a higher octave. At that point, your everyday stress, meaninglessness, frustration, poverty thinking and unnecessary suffering vanish. In their place, abundance, wisdom, inner knowingness, self-trust, and God realization will appear.

The immense heritage from the sages of India can transform your life into your dream life through:

- Meditation techniques
- Sound technology or *mantras*
- Sacred geometry or *yantras*
- Numerology or sacred mathematics
- Yoga poses
- Yogic breathing
- Healing Ayurveda or *science of life*
- Vedic astrology or *science of light*

When I used these tools, my outlook on life and my destiny changed completely. I discovered that we're powerful beyond our wildest dreams, that we're divine beings capable of thought manifestation, and that we're collectively on the verge of discovering our supernormal powers.

Why? Because we're entering a new time of light and human empowerment called by the ancient, intuitive Rishis, *Satya Yuga* or the Golden Age.

Skeptical? Just think of the explosions of yoga, meditation, and non-denominational spiritual groups that can be seen everywhere, even in the most unlikely spaces like businesses, offices, boardrooms, and more.

So I truly believe that spiritual, natural methods can help us develop our potential faster than our most advanced technologies.

Meditation, Vedic astrology and Ayurveda bring us a vast pool of knowledge that answers many human questions and brings easy solutions.

In India, the Tamil Siddha yogis from the state of Tamil Nadu are known as some of the most advanced spiritual scientists the world has ever seen. They are renowned master healers and compassionate supporters of humanity. The masters from this lineage are committed to the well-being and evolution of all human beings.

The Tamil Siddhas know healing and plants in ways we cannot even imagine, and they communicate with the Goddesses or female celestials, which they believe live within the plants. From the Goddesses, they learn the secret ways to turn a plant into a Siddha medicine. They can even ask these celestial beings to preserve and increase the healing powers of the plant after the preparation is completed.

There is well-known literature about how the Siddhas can master their bodies and minds to acquire supernormal powers or siddhis, from which they derive their name.

Stories tell of their capabilities of defying even death by transforming their physical body into a body of light, a process also known as *ascension*.

These spiritual giants remind me of Christ and his incredible miracles. After studying and researching about the Siddhas, I received much validation for my inborn desire to uncover my hidden potential. Their teachings can lead you on a path where there is no place for suffering or ignorance.

My current teacher, Dr. Pillai, is an enlightened Siddha master. Only two years after first meeting him did I realize that I had encountered a real Tamil Siddha. This was a dream come true.

In fact, for long years after reading Paramahansa Yogananda's "Autobiography of a Yogi," I'd been praying to meet a true Siddha master. I wanted to be a student of a Siddha and I did not want to compromise. I knew the secretive Siddhas were not easy to find in our mainstream, modern society.

When a devotee prays intensely to God to know the truth, God sends him a true guru to guide him. This divine grace comes to the student when he demonstrates his desire for liberation.

—PARAMAHANSA YOGANANDA

I remember the day I came across Dr. Pillai's free YouTube videos. It was in 2007: I was working as a certified yoga and meditation teacher, and lived in India. I'd just emailed my wonderful American yoga teacher— Jan Hahuestein—whose traditional yoga school was on the beautiful campus of a Catholic university in Ohio. The spiritual ambiance on campus resembled a hermitage of ancient India, where sages and kings alike received their spiritual and material education.

In her reply to my email, Jan told me that she was heading to the seminar of an Indian spiritual teacher whose name was Dr. Pillai or Dattatreya Shiva Baba. "You can search for his free videos on YouTube."

Immediately after reading her email, I felt compelled to Google his videos. I was both surprised and delighted by the sheer magnitude and profundity of Dr. Pillai's teachings.

I loved all the videos I watched and their content made my heart flutter with desire to meet this teacher.

Then as good luck would have it—when I returned to New York, I came across the homepage of Dr. Pillai's renowned astrological site— AstroVed. There, my eyes fell on an upcoming NYC event in which Dr. Pillai would teach a seminar just a week later. I signed up immediately.

This was synchronicity at its best—I'd just returned to the U.S. and was planning to return to India after a few weeks. So the seminar was scheduled just at the right time. I no longer believe in coincidence, by the way.

The morning of the seminar, I walked into a nondescript hotel conference room already packed with students filling over 70 chairs. There was no particular sign of mystical greatness in this place. I sat down quietly.

But when Dattatreya Siva Baba walked in, a slight figure, simply dressed, silver hair—my mind and body responded with instant bliss. I was unaware of my reaction for a while, and I simply remained calm and alert. Yet I smiled for the entire duration of the seminar. Even more strangely, my spinal column began vibrating upon seeing him. Waves of peace filled my mind and body.

The vibrations lasted for hours, even after the seminar was over and I was driving home.

On that day, I never thought that I had found my Guru. What I had experienced wasn't an intellectual process—but rather a gentle, joyful calmness, and immense inspiration.

Then I began studying with this teacher on a regular basis. It wasn't long before my life began changing in miraculous ways. I took his online programs and went to see him in India every year for his birthday.

Finally, my life became more fulfilling and my work and studies acquired meaning and purpose. I still wanted to evolve and help others do the same. I began to understand how I could accomplish that. This was one of the miracles Dr. Pillai brought me.

Until that moment, my work as a teacher of meditation, yoga, Reiki and Ayurveda had felt incomplete. I'd worked immensely hard, and studied so deeply for over two decades, still feeling ignorant, incapable of finding a fitting channel to integrate my knowledge and inspire my students.

Teaching yoga in the U.S. had been unfulfilling—and I was neither an ashram dweller nor a modern yoga instructor. I couldn't reach the perfect combination of those lifestyles that would fit my vision. I wanted to stay away from restrictive mystical traditions and asceticism in which I didn't belong. Yet I wanted to explore different traditions and find what worked for my individuality and me.

I was dissatisfied with the Vinyasa yoga style being taught in most yoga studios and felt that our Western search for a quick fix had changed yoga in ways that didn't meet my standards. For me, yoga was best defined in the words of Dr. Pillai: "Yoga is not exercise. It's expanding the mind to merge into the divine mind." Yes, as a byproduct we can also attain a beautiful, fit body.

I wanted to help my students experience the joys of discovering their higher self. I knew that in that process they would also achieve perfect health, and joy, as I had.

I wanted them to experience through meditative techniques happiness, healing and inspiration.

In my teachings, I would integrate the yoga poses with a 10-minute final meditation. Still, I felt that something was missing, as my dream was to help my students become truly empowered and able to solve their problems by self-discovery.

Later, I had better luck teaching traditional Yoga Nidra, a deep-relaxation technique of meditation.

So after my usual yoga class, I would spend 30 extra minutes teaching free "yogic sleep" and received raving testimonials from my students. They told me that they experience better results in their studies and higher test scores in their exams. Moreover, they experienced joy and peace throughout the day, their night's sleep improved, and they healed negative emotions.

After these experiences, I began adding a Yoga Nidra practice to all my classes, and the attendance vastly increased. I realized then that people craved and needed bliss.

A real karma yogi, who first acquires knowledge and then works for the welfare of people, quite naturally becomes popular and famous. There is no enemy of such a man but even if there are, he is able to vanquish them. His popularity in the society increases on account of his successes and good deeds.

—SAMA VEDA

CHAPTER 2

Your Celestial Origins

The universe is not outside of you. Look inside yourself; everything that you want, you already are.

—RUMI

Divine consciousness is embedded in you. This may seem like an exaggeration, primarily because we aren't being taught how to tap into our spiritual potential, which includes supernormal powers. A university course in a school of divinity can teach you about comparing wisdom traditions, and that's about it.

I recall that in 2004 I came across studies from Duke University and Yale that explained the benefits of *Yoga Nidra* or yogic sleep. Yogic sleep practice leads to a deep state of relaxation—from alpha to theta brain waves. Scientists have found amazing healing can result from this practice.

More scientific research was also done in the 1990s on the brain of a yogi, Swami Rama, whose spiritual tradition had a great impact on my training as a yoga teacher.

Swami Rama could control his brain, its brainwaves, and states of consciousness. He could easily enter the beta, alpha, theta and delta states successfully and just by planning to do so.

He would stun the doctors conducting the study that he would enter consecutively each state for five minutes, accomplishing this with no apparent effort. He once deliberately stopped his heart. Worried that he had died, the scientists intervened and forced him to return to his normal breathing state. Needless to say, Swami Rama did so, and proven to be both alive and healthy.

His proven yogic powers had fascinated me during the time of my yoga certification studies, and still do. Published records prove that Swami Rama had acquired complete control over his autonomic nervous system and other bodily functions, along with the complete mastery of his consciousness.

The EKG recorded 17 seconds of atrial flutter, during which the blood in Swami Rama's body stopped flowing... But Swami Rama was not meditating when he raised his heart rate nor when he produced different brain waves for the EEG.

For eons, the yogis have maintained that yogic sleep and other meditation techniques can stimulate unused parts of the brain connected with expanded awareness, higher consciousness, and wish-fulfillment.

These same spiritual masters have maintained for eons that our origins are divine. It is unfortunate that in our waking state we seldom think of the Divine, and we hide our longing for spiritual fulfillment under layers of stress, confusion, daily tasks, fearful thoughts, overthinking, self-doubt, misinformation, distractions, delays, frustration and sorrow.

Again, the intuitive Rishis taught that inborn qualities are both unlimited potential and bliss. Without the dawning of this truth, our lives risk remaining either meaningless or unfulfilling.

So we can regain our inborn knowledge and practice thought manifestation: meditation and special mantras or sounds are some of the tools that can help you attain that desirable ability. You will find some of these techniques in the chapters about the 12 Spiritual Laws.

Instant manifestation and fast time go beyond our concepts of linear time, which requires planning, implementing, and long waiting for results.

I love what Dr. Pillai's says about time, *"Waiting is a waste of time."* This has become my opinion, too. We all know how painful it is to wait for our dreams to come true, to see the positive results of decades of work and goals. 'Waiting is a waste of time' appealed to me when I felt that my evolution was taking too long and that I wanted results and solutions.

I truly believe that you don't need to settle for a mediocre job, relationship, lifestyle, and lack of happiness. Life is meant to be joyful and effortless, and this is our collective destiny and upgrade.

Soon you'll also see why divine synchronicity has brought you here. You were chosen to leave your mark in the world, and you can even help future generations experience their next stage of human evolution through finding your purpose. I will help you learn how in the upcoming chapters.

CHAPTER 3

A Spiritual Solution to Human Problems

The Goddess gives you super intelligence and miraculous powers.
—DR. PILLAI

S ome fantastic and most useful aspects of Vedic astrology help you identify auspicious times for your manifestations. These time windows are known as *time shaktis*—or power times, which can help you plan your activities when the benevolent Goddess archetype of immense compassion and love is present. She is believed to bring miracles and wish fulfillment. *Shakti* is the energy of the Divine Feminine and a fundamental aspect of creation.

In ancient times, all the kings of India consulted astrologers, and even hosting them permanently in the royal palace along with other dignitaries. Today, Vedic astrology is still routinely used before marriages, inaugurations, business launches, and financial investments.

The Goddess and My Guru's Blessings

The woman is the Creatress, regardless whether she is the human woman or the archetypal Divine Woman. The feminine itself is sacred, the Mother Goddess. Without the woman, there is no creation. So the feminine energy is the most powerful energy.
—DR. PILLAI

Once I was fortunate to practice Yoga Nidra with Dr. Pillai in Rameshwaram, a sacred town in Tamil Nadu, India. He guided a group of students through a deep practice of yogic sleep. The large room's floor was packed with people lying on their yoga mats.

During that 3-hour practice—which felt like 30 minutes—I floated in and out of galaxies. I then saw a most beautiful Goddess, my favorite celestial being since Dr. Pillai had given me her name as a spiritual name. I knew that she was the supreme Divine Mother, Lalitha Tripura Sundari. She smiled and took me into the Sri Chakra or Sri Yantra, a sacred, geometrical representation of the Goddess. From the Sri Chakra, she took me throughout the universe. Everything was orderly, peaceful and luminous.

She also revealed secrets of the cosmos and the Sri Chakra—in the center of which there was a sacred point, called *bindu*, considered her seat. I also learned that the bindu was a portal into other dimensions.

The Goddess then said that the Sri Chakra was a hologram of the cosmos.

At the end of that Yoga Nidra practice, I got up with an incredible knowingness about my future and how it would unfold—I had plans in place and not a shred of doubt that I would succeed. This was a life-changing experience that has remained with me ever since. That was the power of Dr. Pillai's blessings.

I felt, however, the need to double check and googled the information I had learned about the Sri Chakra. I then found some spiritual literature that confirmed what the Goddess has said. In fact, throughout the millennia, the Sri Chakra has been considered a holographic representation of the universe.

CHAPTER 4

How I Uncovered My Spiritual Self

Although my parents weren't spiritual or religious, I became fascinated with the Gospels and Jesus' miracle stories around age 6 or 7. I found books of these stories in the house of my maternal grandmother. I can still see her tall figure, erect posture, head held high, elegantly dressed. Her demeanor appeared stern and aloof, which didn't reveal her true nature.

In fact, she was both incredibly spiritual, and a very righteous and charitable woman. When she became a widow, her adult children began scolding her because she often donated large sums of money to the poor.

When I visited her, I read and reread the miracle stories. For me, those sacred tales were more real than my schoolbooks. And I took for granted others would take miracles seriously too. When I realized that adults and peers were more skeptical than believers, I was hurt and felt that they just didn't understand the secrets of life.

At that time, I regularly talked to angels and Jesus, and for me, they were more present than my own siblings. More recently in a meditation guided by my teacher Dr. Pillai, I saw Jesus—and suddenly a childhood memory came to me. I remembered that Jesus would appear to me when I was very young, about 4 or 5 years old. He would smile and play with me. That memory brought me tears of joy, and incredible longing for His love.

At nine, my mother began teaching me Latin. This is significant because then, I started loving stories about ancient Rome and its myths. At that same age, I thought that one day I would become an archeologist and dig deeper into the mysteries of our past. To me, life was a miracle and I couldn't understand why others didn't care for God.

I was introverted and compassionate. I couldn't stand watching how badly some people treated the poor or gossiped about others. I felt their pain.

My mother was afraid that others would take advantage of my sensitivity. "After looking into your eyes, they'll see how caring you are and they'll exploit you," she often said with some harshness. I now realize that she owned that same quality, felt it was a weakness, and was trying to protect me.

Fortunately, I didn't believe her fear and I was never exploited—at least not as a child or adolescent.

Spiritual Detour

Then when I was 12, my sister died in an accident. That same day, I lost my faith and stopped praying for many years.

Yet I always tried to expand my horizon and knowledge, loved poetry the most and spending time alone reading. I barely slept as I read until dawn, even on school nights.

I didn't feel any pressure to fit in. I loved classical music and detested the Rolling Stones—whom most of my friends adored. As a child, I loved the Beatles. As a teen, I was repulsed by the Rolling Stones' harsh lyrics and metallic-sounding music. I'd rather go to the symphony with my parents and their adult friends.

I was bored with living in Italy, too. I wanted to see the world and how other populations lived. So I studied languages. As a teenager, I went to Paris and London to shop, because Italian fashion and everything else in my country seemed boring. I'd also borrow my mother's silk blouses to wear with jeans. She had beautiful clothes.

Yoga as Antidote to Sadness

In my adolescence, I began my philosophy and literature studies, and became very disappointed with those teachings, and somewhat confused. I couldn't find adequate explanations for objective reality— only infinite theories and philosophers arguing with each other. Other students seemed satisfied with inconclusive answers. I wasn't. I felt sad because neither philosophers, nor academics, nor authors had given me satisfactory explanations about the nature of God, the meaning of life, and other aspects of metaphysics that I intuitively knew to be true.

I comforted myself with art history and classical music. Among the Italian cities, my two great loves were Rome and Venice, and the magnificent works of art by Tiepolo, Titian, Caravaggio, Botticelli, and Bernini.

My family and I spent our summers in Rome in my parents' condo. At that time, my mother was a journalist for the Roman daily *Il Popolo*.

The reason for loving Rome is self-explanatory—the ancient ruins, the ubiquitous churches, the sunset behind the seven hills, that feeling that nothing is permanent or truly important could seduce a visitor forever. But I disliked its noisy streets.

So, falling in love with Rome, always felt a bit painful: like falling madly in love with a debauched man. His stubble, unkempt clothes would keep you on edge, and you knew you couldn't rely on this person for the long haul.

Whereas, after growing up in Bergamo—originally a Venetian republic resembling a peaceful, slow-paced Swiss mountain town, I fell in love with Venice. There, I felt comfortable being sad and reserved—the way I usually was. Its mysterious, little streets or *calle* appealed to my sensibility and esthetic. My art studies found complete fulfillment in Venice.

In Rome, something seemed to go amiss in the chaotic traffic and hordes of visitors. Its emptiness in the summer made it look like a ghost town that you love but also scares you. Wandering tourists in blinding sun were the only signs of life after most Romans had escaped to beach or mountain resorts. I always felt that the light was too bright, harsh on my eyes, and that I was dressed too warm for any season.

In Venice, even a pauper looked like a prince. An obscure writer held the same status of a Nobel Prize winner. Exquisitely beautiful art and ordinary objects stood out majestically in soft light and humid mist. Local women wore conservative yet elegant styles. There was a certain reserve that appealed to my shyness. At that time, I loved the feeling of poetic sadness that Venice evoked. I now realize that I was simply depressed. And I longed for more freedom from my parents' supervision and beliefs.

What did you love to do as a child? I could read or write for hours, forgetting time, hunger, thirst and other people. Yet unlike my famous mother, who was well known for her journalistic talent, I imagined my future in a traditional marriage, surrounded by loved ones and lots of children. Still, writing was my passion. I just didn't want to do it professionally—but just for fun. Then at 20, I caved in and at the request of some editors, who thought that I had inherited my mother's way with words, I began contributing as a freelancer to travel and literary magazines. My passions for literature, travel and foreign cultures would later prove very helpful in understanding others, their unique hopes, fears and outlooks.

I found people around the world to be amazing in both their differences and similarities. I often felt surprised or uplifted. Now I think that all the time my soul was training me for what I do now—in fact I love to help people uncover their spiritual self, and teach how to solve everyday problems—the *yogic way*.

I also believe that happiness is a very important pursuit in life. Even if your purpose includes service—it would be impossible to do so from a state of misery and frustration.

I've always felt that there was a common thread that unites us all: as we all have similar wishes—being happy, being loved, learning, being connected, prospering, and creating. And most of us invoke the Divine, although in different names and forms. Yet at the core, there is the same spiritual seeking.

Maharishi Mahesh Yogi, the Guru of the Beatles and one of Dr. Pillai's teachers, used to say that we must be very, very happy—at all times.

And I've discovered that when you make your happiness your priority, you can also purposefully serve others and make a difference, because when you're happy you contribute to others' happiness.

I slept and dreamt that life was joy. I awoke and saw that life was service. I acted and behold, service was joy.

—RABINDRANATH TAGORE

Ancient Religious Art and Literature

The true work of art is but a shadow of the divine perfection.

—MICHELANGELO

What is your great passion? Is it possible that this passion is showing you a hidden path to happiness? Could you make a living through that? And if you didn't need to work for a living would you pursue it all the time? You need to find what that unstoppable passion is, if you're clear. Today—I can see how my path, although it looked rocky at times, working at jobs that were very stressful, in reality, was a seamless fabric of events that led me to my purpose and what I do today: coaching and teaching spiritual tools for happiness.

Since childhood, I had a great passion for Italian religious art of the 1300s and Renaissance. I adored the paintings and statues of the beautiful Mother Mary in a blue veil or the tiny *puttini* or little angelic figures near baby Jesus. I loved the skies, nature and stars in daylight. The paintings looked divine.

As a teen, to secular philosophy and literature, I preferred biographies of mystics and stories of their supernormal powers. I loved philosophy books by *Saint Augustine,* and stories about *Saint Francis,* and saints who could levitate in a halo of light, experiencing ecstasy. I wanted to experience those states of grace, too. But I didn't like monastic life—of that, I was certain.

Slowly in my 20s, I began believing in God again. I also realized that we live in a just universe. Still, I didn't want to go to church.

Despite knowing that our planet was often devastated by wars, injustice and pain, I had an intuitive knowing that the cosmos was both orderly and perfect.

A decade or so later, my yogic studies confirmed this early inner vision: the universe is embedded in justice, order and love. Righteousness wins, good triumphs over evil, and spiritual evolution is never-ending. Then, my faith in God grew in leaps and bounds.

CHAPTER 5

Tap into Your Hidden Powers

Reincarnation occurs because we decide that we haven't learned enough lessons.

—SYLVIA BROWNE

Your spiritual awakening doesn't need to be difficult. In this book, you will find the inspiration, real-life stories and guidance from someone who has made her purpose the number one priority: making mistakes, experiencing detours, studying too much, and sometimes experiencing a life that was all work and no bliss.

While the rewards were priceless, I cannot say that spiritual growth needs to be that painful or hard. I've now found a better balance: a 200 percent life that Dr. Pillai talks about: 100 percent spiritual fulfillment, and 100 percent material fulfillment. So you can have the new car, you don't need to eat only tasteless rice and fast for prolonged periods of time. There's no need to spend 12 hours in meditation or chanting (yes, I've done that too).

A common argument against spirituality is that you need be a secluded ascetic and live a miserable life of renunciation.

This is not what the Siddhas teach. These yogis and masters prioritize studying the self, loving God, helping others, yet don't necessarily live like ascetics. Rather they can get married, have children, and master thought manifestation. And they enjoy both nature and perfect health.

I can assure you that spiritual awakening can happen in an instant, as long as you believe that you are powerful, remain in a state of unconditional love, self-restraint, allow change and empower yourself to challenge difficult karma: just because you were unhappy yesterday, doesn't mean that you need remain the same today.

Stay alert, express your creativity, change your mindset and allow God into your life. Allow yourself to listen to beautiful, melodious music. You can find studies on sound frequencies, and how some sounds can

21

kill plants, and others can make plants thrive and grow. Similarly, some melodies open your heart chakra or energy center, heal your emotions, and lead to you to bliss.

In later chapters, I will show you how to use certain sounds that can help you manifest your best life.

I so wish I'd met my spiritual teachers in my teens, and received the step-by-step spiritual guidance that my soul craved. Have you ever asked yourself: "Why am I here, and what is my purpose?"

These questions are starting points to a better life—because they lead to uncovering your true, divine nature, so you can have the authentic and blissful life you wish for. Moreover, when you learn to listen to your higher, spiritual self, you'll be guided to healing yourself, the earth and all of life. My consciousness shifted at the time I learned from a classical Ayurvedic text that the entire universe cheers when you heal yourself. And, more importantly, all beings and the entire universe benefit from your healing.

When you take care of your health, choose a lifestyle that is suitable to your unique mind-body, a routine that includes early morning walks, meditation, eating fresh foods that nourish you, the results are bubbling joy, enhanced intelligence of the body and mind, positive emotions, resilience to stress, and a stronger immune system. The final result is perfect health.

Additionally, the mind awakens, and you experience both calmness and alertness. At the Maharishi School of Management in Iowa, for example, when the staff began serving to students freshly made organic vegetarian foods, replacing the usual cafeteria meals, students became more alert, their test scores were higher and depression disappeared among both students and staff.

You feel energetic and vital. Plus, your enthusiasm for life returns. Then you could also choose music that heals you and doesn't stress you. You'll become more attuned to what helps you grow and thrive. The universe, in fact, is orchestrating your evolution and healing at all times.

If you're reading this book, you too are likely to feel a stirring in your heart, longing for God, desire to express your higher potential— and live in a heaven on earth, which you intuitively know it's possible.

Did you know that your spiritual awakening is helpful to all? It isn't self-indulgent to spend time exploring your higher, spiritual self.

When you engage in learning more about how to cater to your true needs for lightheartedness, innocence, openness, sincere love, creativity, dance, music, spiritual bliss, you will be much happier and more successful. More importantly, you will also contribute to the Earth's blissful passage from darkness or *Kali Yuga* to the era of light or *Satya Yuga*. Our collective entrance into a new era through an evolutionary shift was predicted by the yogis of India thousands of years ago. There are also mentions of this collective, spiritual upgrade in the predictions within other world religions.

I believe that our current, busy and chaotic lifestyles, under the hypnotic effects of repetitive, sensational, dramatic news broadcasts from nearly every corner is robbing us of the inner silence we need to thrive and our spiritual powers. I find that people often feel more loneliness, regret and confusion due to constant stress and lack of authentic living. For most of us, it's hard to find a peaceful haven to get in touch with our humanness and creativity.

Maybe you're now feeling simultaneously unhappy with several aspects of your life—suffering from an incompatible relationship, being overweight or out of shape, or disconnected from your family, peers and friends.

Your sensitivity and frustration are both valid, and a prerequisite for your transformation. We often need to feel the pain and reach a point where we cannot take another day like that before we can find a permanent solution. You might feel that you can no longer accept a life unworthy of you. Suffering has an uncanny quality: it can make you believe that you'll never be happy again. And too often, you might feel hopeless.

In my experience—a permanent way out of these terrible ups and downs is through spiritual self-referral. When you learn self-referral, you won't believe the distorted, negative reality that surfaces from media or unconscious individuals.

Self-referral, trusting yourself and your authentic desires will help you invest in yourself. Coaching, retreats, self-expression, creativity, goal setting, fulfillment of desires, finding your true purpose, and helping others can bring you wonderful byproducts: lasting well-being, meaning, joy, love, spiritual growth, and bliss.

You can naturally make a small shift and acquire a new perspective: you're infinitely powerful. This new outlook can empower you and help you move away from a limited existence to your dream life.

God doesn't need to have a reason to help you. He helps you regardless, whether you are reasonable or unreasonable. Just keep asking with 100 percent faith.

—DR. BASKARAN PILLAI

How to Shine Forth Your Inner Divinity

Do you remember your childhood dreams, and the incredible joy you felt playing with your friends, and engaging in your favorite activities? The spiritual masters tell us that we are supposed to live happily all the time. Even after a loss, we can return to joy, knowing that everything is in Divine, perfect order.

God is not at all a strict, scary being who wants to punish you. In the Indian scriptures, *Krishna* gives his love, plays the flute and truly enjoys his time with people, the *Gopis* or female devotees, and the incredibly beautiful *Radha*—his favorite devotee.

What is your vision of God? Maybe it's time that we can rethink what we have been taught about God, especially if it doesn't fit our inner knowingness that God is love. In fact, as Dr. Pillai says, *"Love is God."*

The superman expands his life energy and consciousness from his body into all space, feeling as his own self the presence of universes in the vast cosmos, as well as every minute atom of the earth.

—PARAMAHANSA YOGANANDA

My First Astrological Reading

Our lives are filled with synchronicity. Wouldn't you love noticing it? Or perhaps you're already aware of the interconnectedness of life—a connected universe where there are no coincidences, but only perfect synchronicities.

I was barely 20 when I first met a Vedic astrologer while traveling in India. I was staying at a beautiful hotel in Bombay across from the majestic Gate of India. In the hallways, tall white columns gave way to lovely moldings on the pastel-colored walls. The uniformed staff resembled more the Indian royals of colonial times than hotel employees: the men wore sparkling white jackets with gold buttons and a pink or white turban. The women donned beautiful saris in subdued colors and lovely smiles, their lucent black hair neatly tied up in a perfect chignon. This scene reminded to me of illustrations I had seen of old India, reconstructed in perfect style in the 1980s.

I entered the astrologer's room. I remember the high ceilings and bright white walls. Everything was filled with light and that's all I remember of the décor. The astrologer too, was wearing whites and sported a short beard and hair slightly reaching his shoulders. I thought he was about my age.

Soon after he began the reading, I was stunned at the accuracy of his analysis of my birth chart. He seemed to know my past and came up with specific events that no one else could have known other than my parents. He also said, "You write short stories," which was true. I then learned that he was giving me so many details of my life to confirm the correct time of my birth, so that his predictions could also be accurate. I confirmed everything.

Then he told me about a significant episode of my childhood: the death of my sister. He told me that my childhood had been "sad, very sad." This was all true yet due to my shyness, I never revealed that truth to my friends or anyone else. It was incredibly liberating that someone was acknowledging my suffering.

This chart reading explained all my peculiarities. I remained silent and pensive. He wrote down the predictions: they all came to pass over the years.

Little did I know that over a decade later, I'd embark on my yogic studies and would eventually develop a great passion for Vedic astrology—which I believe is a must if you want to understand yourself, your life, and the world.

Vedic astrology explained the strange synchronicities in my life, my likes and dislikes. So I began a full immersion in the Vedic sciences that is still going on today—these subjects are oceans of knowledge.

Karma is not a superstition—it's the law of cause and effect that brings the positive, neutral and negative consequences of our actions. It's the science of time and how you can predict what will happen in your relationship, what kind of partner you'll meet, the career you'll be drawn to and the amount of success you will experience. Even better: it teaches you how to overcome hurdles and provides you with remedies to fix your problems and receive miracles.

CHAPTER 6

Rishis, Siddhas and Vedic Astrology

- *The Earth goes around the Sun*—RIG VEDA 10. 22. 14
- *The Sun neither rises nor sets*—ATRAYA BRAHMAN 3˙44
- *The Sun and the whole universe are round*—YAJUR VEDA
- *There are many suns*—RIG VEDA 9. 114. 3
- *There are seven colors in the Sun*—ATHARVA VEDA 7. 107. 1

The short meditations and powerful affirmations in *Bliss Lab* can help you make the small shift you need to challenge a mediocre life and live one that you love. You may find that when you look at yourself in the mirror after a few minutes of meditation or affirmation practice—a lovely change in your facial expression occurs. In fact, you might see a younger, more relaxed, and more attractive you.

I've experienced this. For example, I was surprised when after guiding my students in a meditation class, they appeared both younger and happier. They looked the way one does after a prolonged vacation or when falling in love—joyful, bright-eyed, and radiating a healthy glow.

Planets and Stars are Conscious

Miracles are not in the domain of Gods. They are in your own domain and how you're going to connect your brain to the stars.

—DR. PILLAI

Have you ever looked at the night sky, wondering whether you had a connection with the stars? Or spent a summer night wishing to learn the secrets of the cosmos? Many have written sublime poems about the

Sun and the Moon and we have, of course, technology that is meant to explore space. Still, many questions remain.

Many Indian scholars believe that around 10,000 BC, the Rishis uncovered mysteries of the stars, planets and human consciousness. Some of their knowledge was later written in the form of verses in the four *Vedas*. The *Vedic* people were said to live in North India—in today's state of *Haryana*—near a large body of water called the *Saraswati River*, which was mentioned in the Rig Veda, the oldest Veda.

But Western scholars and historians made objections to those dates and even the existence of that river because the river could not be found. Yet recently, satellite images of this area have revealed evidence of an ancient river in that exact location.

Moreover, the yogis and Siddhas of that period were said to have acquired supernormal powers of intuition, prediction, manifestation, teleportation, breath control, changing their bodies into light and conquering death, to mention just a few. Additionally, they studied the cosmos and traveled through space in their astral bodies during advanced states of meditation.

The Vedic seers also invented a scientific system of prediction based on the stars and planets called *Jyotisha*—from *jyoti* or light, and Isha or God. So, Vedic astrology sheds divine light on your future, your karma, and shows the blueprint of your soul through many rebirths.

This science or art is called a *vedanga,* or an addition to the Vedas and auxiliary science that favors human evolution, lasting happiness and the healing of human sorrow.

Nature and stars are more connected to you than you think. In Indian spiritual texts, you can find a great explanation of this in the verse *Yat Pinde Tat Brahmande*—which means that man is made of the same elements as the universe. In other words, you and the universe are one.

Men should take their knowledge from the sun, the moon and the stars.

—RALPH WALDO EMERSON

The intuitive seers wrote extensively about the wonders of the cosmos—from both the astronomical and spiritual points of view. This predictive system shows the reasons for your birth on this planet at this time.

The Rishis' understanding of the human brain and consciousness was extremely advanced. They even designed and described flying machines called *Vimanas* meant to travel into space.

Each of the nine celestial bodies that we observe in Vedic astrology is a massive source of consciousness with definite characteristics. This knowledge can be used every day as a practical guide to fixing your problems—big or small.

Vedic astrology is the science of time. Everyone wants to know what's going to happen on a daily basis. The planets are the energy behind the happenings in a person's life, city or even country.

—DR. PILLAI

CHAPTER 7

Miracles by the Spiritual Masters

Let noble thoughts come to us from all sides.

—RIG VEDA

I was standing outdoors and looking into the eyes of a white horse. I caressed her head and neck. Her white coat beamed with pure white light. I knew this magnificent animal was very sick and needed a lot of love to heal. I tenderly put my arms around her neck.

In the morning, I awoke from this dream and wondered about its meaning. I didn't own a white horse. Believing that it was a meaningful dream, I wrote it down in a journal.

A few days later, Paola, an acquaintance from Rome, phoned me that she'd just arrived in Chicago, where I lived at the time. We agreed to meet and I invited her to my house.

A mutual dear friend from France had put us in touch. Paola told about herself, her travels, Rome—where I also used to live—and we chatted about our common French friend.

"Do you want to go and meet *Amma* tomorrow?" she suddenly asked. I said that I didn't know that name. "She's an Indian saint who hugs people and who's now touring the U.S. I'm going to meet her here in Chicago." The idea aroused my curiosity, so I agreed to accompany her and offered to drive.

The next day I drove and picked up Paola, we left the North Shore and drove to a Western suburb I'd never heard of.

We got lost several times. We tried again and again to get better directions—there was no GPS at the time. But on the road, strange coincidences or synchronicities happened. Signs with reassuring words like peace and divine appeared here and there.

Then we stopped for a quick lunch at a fast food restaurant. As we were sitting and eating our sandwiches, two ethereal looking girls dressed in white entered. They were escorting a large group of female little children. They all sat and ate their lunches.

A few minutes later, an adolescent boy also dressed in white came with a group of little boys. They ordered drinks and food and also sat. I knew that these young people were somehow connected with Amma and her organization. The hotel we were looking for must have been close by.

When we finally reached the hotel, an usher directed us to a huge, crowded ballroom. Most women and men there wore white—and their faces looked calm and content. Everyone seemed to be in a state of bliss.

Something in that place stirred unknown emotions in me and I suddenly began crying. Not a few tears, but actual sobbing for a few minutes, until I realized that my chest felt lighter as if a large rock had been lifted. It was for me a new emotion. I wasn't sad at all, just peaceful. My tears must have been noticed by the white clad staff, because a woman approached me and asked softly: "Is this your first time?" There was genuine concern in her tone. I said "Yes."

She gently pushed me in front of the long line of people and I saw a dark-skinned woman wearing a white sari. She was surrounded by tens of people sitting at her feet. I was confused. Then she, Amma, looked at me with concern in her eyes. With an incredibly sweet smile, she reached out to me with her arms. She held me on her chest and I began sobbing again. She spoke in my ear—I didn't understand. Someone asked me what was my original language—Amma started whispering comforting Italian words, even though I spoke fluent English. It worked, and I stopped crying.

Then I remembered the dream. I realized that it had been a premonition of this extraordinary encounter with a saint I'd never met before. Clearly, I was in the process of healing some deep wounds I didn't even know I had. I was the horse.

Later on that day, I noticed a large picture of an Indian *god* hanging from a wall. "It's *Krishna*," Paola told me. "The cows are symbols of the human souls." So the horse in the dream was actually a cow. I guessed that I was receiving the blessings of this god, Krishna. My dream had alerted me about an important spiritual experience and encounter with the Saint. I remained peaceful for the entire day.

Finally, I understood how everything had conspired to fulfill my need for transformation. It wasn't an intellectual process at all—it seemed magical.

Faith is what is going to heal, or fix a situation that you want to correct.

—DR. PILLAI

The Power of Intuition

Mysticism is the ultimate knowledge, the ultimate wisdom that everyone must use to exercise his full potential.

—DR. PILLAI

I cherish intuitive intelligence and honor it in both myself and others. When you learn to listen to your intuition, you'll find yourself in the right place at the right time. I've had this experience innumerable times and you can, too.

When you listen to your heart, your intuitive faculties will be awakened and you'll naturally resist manipulation or conditioning, which are toxic for your soul. You will better resist negativity from others, because you'll intuitively know that they don't have your best interest at heart, or they are simply unaware of their own divinity.

For example, for some people you are too thin, for others too fat. For some, too outspoken, yet for others too shy. We all know the pain of being given a label that doesn't define us. Your higher potential, in fact, is deeply embedded in your brain, DNA, cells, and soul. All you need to do is peel away the unnecessary layers of limited identifications that cover your divine nature and supernormal abilities.

For instance, the ancient yogis didn't identify themselves with their actions, physical appearance, social background, associations, likes and dislikes, relationships, or skills. They explained the truth of their divine nature with a double negation: "Neti, neti" or "I am not this, nor that."

We often don't see others as they really are—blame it on social and cultural conditioning, lack of time or our limited perceptions. Then we miss the real person behind the appearance.

Wouldn't it be wonderful if you could express yourself more authentically? If one could communicate for example: "I only work as a school teacher (or lawyer, artist, nurse, engineer, and so on). I like to paint, have three brothers and once I won a state tennis competition. But I'm actually an infinite being with amazing potential, immense love, and a great passion for making a difference in the world."

Can you imagine an ancient yogi attending a modern gathering where people immediately exchange their professional credentials? *"Hello, I live in a cave where I sit all day for 15 hours, trying to realize that I'm God. I also scout the cosmos in my meditations, and I've learned that we're all interconnected."*

As paradoxical as this sounds, I believe that we're all inclined to identify ourselves with our activities, forgetting our true, divine core. Many contemporary artists also talk about the fragmentation of our society. I agree. But the guidance of the spiritual masters can collectively help us awaken from the dream of separation.

Synchronicity and intuition work both in big and small ways to make your life easier. Your life, too, can benefit from noticing and opening up to synchronicity, which will solve many of your everyday problems. Below is a brief example of how it may work for you.

One early morning, as I was driving back from the home of two of my private meditation students, I decided to stop at a local fitness center where I taught yoga several times a week. There was a delay in receiving my paycheck—either the owner wasn't in the office or he was occupied in a meeting or on the phone.

Without knowing why, that early morning I drove to the health club and parked the car in a nearly empty parking lot, even though I wasn't supposed to teach. As I was about to exit my car, another car pulled in next to me. It was the owner of the health club. We said hello and I told him I was looking for him to pick up my paycheck. His reply, "Sure, come on in." And he gave me my check.

This is a simple example to show you how synchronicity is both a product of your intuition and Divine guidance. I went to the gym on a whim—and it's important to note that this episode happened after meditation.

Truly, I say to you, whoever believes in me will also do the works that I do; and greater works than these will he do, because I am going to the Father.

—JOHN 14:12

CHAPTER 8

Timeless Spiritual Tools to Bring Heaven on Earth

If the doors of perception were cleansed, everything would appear to man as it is, Infinite. For man has closed himself up, till he sees all things through narrow chinks of his cavern.

—WILLIAM BLAKE

Myths and Archetypes

Myths are eternal realities. Your subconscious mind can make sense of them. They explain ancient knowledge and positive thought forms in symbols, and the mind understands these symbols instantaneously without the help of rational thinking or long explanations.

Some myths have been found to be rooted in actual historical events—as in the story of Lord Rama, a royal warrior who became an archetype of perfection in his roles as the ideal son, ideal king, ideal husband, and ideal brother. In the Indian epic Ramayana, the cities mentioned in its events have been found through archeological excavations. The town of Rameshwaram in Tamil Nadu, where Rama stopped to perform karma removal rituals still exists. And the bridge from South India to Sri Lanka—once believed to be fiction—can now be identified through satellite images as it had sunk into the ocean thousands of years ago.

The American scholar Joseph Campbell and the Swiss psychiatrist Carl Jung have talked extensively about the importance of archetypes.

Archetypes include the Gods and Goddesses of India. These benevolent celestial beings can awaken dormant powers within your brain and consciousness.

Dr. Pillai says that these gods are not mere ideas, but rather they also have a tridimensional body. And although they live in the subtle planes (or different galaxies), they sometimes take on a human form to communicate with humans.

The contents of the collective unconscious are archetypes, primordial images that reflect basic patterns that are common to us all, and which have existed universally since the dawn of time.

—CARL JUNG

How to Connect with Archetypes

Food offerings are critical. Offering food to a statue of a deity or archetype can do a lot of good, and it's not just a superstition. These Gods and Goddesses do exist.

—DR. PILLAI

- *Look at images of celestial archetypes*

Looking at images of Lakshmi, Vishnu, Hanuman, Saturn, Venus, or Shiva, for example, can enhance your spiritual practice and shift your consciousness in very positive ways. Neuroscientists Dr. Andrew Newberg and Mark Waldman, who have conducted extensive research, have written the book, *How God Changes Your Brain*. They said, for instance, that looking at an image of Ganesha—the Indian elephant-headed archetype—in just a few minutes can activate different parts of your brain that lead to higher intelligence and compassion.

- *Explore myths and research an archetype*

Notice the archetypes' attributes you would like for yourself and their supernormal powers. Try communicating with them and observe the kinds of thoughts that arise in your mind.

- *Be loving*

In general, treating an archetype like a real human being—always with love, respect and even praise—can bring you their blessings in the form of a different mindset or an outright miracle—a helpful intervention from another person, or a sudden, positive event.

- *Offer foods and other items to their images*

When you treat benevolent archetypes like living beings, you create a mutual relationship—in a process called in Sanskrit *parasparam* or reciprocity. You take care of them, and they, in turn, take care of you by fulfilling your wishes.

- *Call them by their traditional mantra or sound waves*

A mantra is said to protect the mind from negativity or bad karmic thoughts. Mantras are considered super sounds that can change your mindset from negative to positive.

- *Wear their traditional colors*

Colors are frequencies as they vibrate at different speeds, evoking different moods and thought patterns. There is research you can find on the effects of colors on the mind.

- *Feed them*

Sweets and vegetarian foods are best.

Example of How to Connect with an Archetypal Being

To invoke and honor Goddess Lakshmi, the archetype of immense wealth, beauty and happiness, call her and praise her with her mantras, feed her, honor her, and ask for miracles. Thank her with sincerity.

Recite
- Shreem Brzee 108 times
- Shreem 108 times
- Or another Lakshmi mantra

Wear
- Clean, well-pressed clothes
- New clothes
- White or pink clothes

Offer
- Chocolate
- Sweet juicy fruits
- Sweet dried fruits (raisins, dates)
- *Khir* or rice pudding
- Milk
- Honey
- Tulsi leaves
- Raw rice mixed with turmeric powder
- Pink roses

- Pink lotus flowers
- A cup of fresh water

When offering any prayers or foods to the archetypes, it's paramount to do so with love and positive emotions. Your emotions are more powerful than your thoughts.

You have to fall from the head to the heart, and manifest from the heart.

—DR. PILLAI

Yantras or Sacred Geometry

According to the Vedas, geometry is a vibration. A *yantra* is a super tool for manifestation thanks to its sacred designs and inscriptions. Yantras can be geometrical representations of a planet, a constellation, the cosmos, a sacred sound or mantra, or benevolent celestial beings with miraculous powers.

A yantra has a special design that is usually inscribed on a metal plate and is made with sacred proportions. This device is believed to help you manifest your wishes: more money, a happy relationship, well-being and even enlightenment.

Dr. Pillai says that a yantra is a technology and a machine that radiates positive vibrations. These vibrations have the potential to work on your own brain waves and change your consciousness.

Yantras accelerate your achievements—on both the material and spiritual levels. Their encoded messages work silently on your thoughts and remove negativity, which will speed your desired manifestations. A yantra can even accelerate your spiritual evolution and bring you permanent bliss.

For example, there are yantras for Lakshmi, the *Goddess* archetype of wealth, or the elephant-headed archetype *Ganesha* that removes all kinds of obstacles—from the present, past and future. There is also a *Vishnu* yantra, the celestial archetype that sustains the universe.

The *Sri Chakra yantra* is particularly powerful. It represents the celestial Goddess archetype Shri Lalita or Tripura Sundari, meaning the most beautiful in the three worlds. This archetype is considered the Supreme Divine Mother. Contentment, beauty, positivity, love, and enjoyment of one's life are common results from using the Sri Chakra, which can also lead you to spiritual enlightenment.

The Goddess is the miracle-performing intelligence within the brain called 'Arul Shakti,' or 'Chit Shakti.' 'Chit' means supernormal consciousness, which is the consciousness to do anything, to know anything, and to be anywhere, anytime.

—DR. PILLAI

How to Use a Yantra

To activate a yantra, you can pour clean water on it and then pour some cold milk. Rinse it with water again, and pat it dry with a clean cloth. Keep it on a clean altar or shelf. You can place fresh flowers on it and offer a light—in the form of an oil or ghee lamp, or a candle and incense. Then you can meditate in front of it.

It's believed that by using a yantra we are able to change the past and influence the future. Imagine if you could undo a mistake you made a few years ago that cost you a relationship or a large amount of money.

A wealth yantra, for example, could help you recover your money. A relationship yantra can bring you a better relationship by positively affecting your consciousness and body to resonate with positive vibrations.

In the universe, there are things that are known, and things that are unknown, and in between, there are doors.

—WILLIAM BLAKE

Mantras are the building blocks of matter.

—DR. PILLAI

The most powerful words for creation are sacred sounds called *mantras*—usually, these syllables represent the names of the Indian gods or archetypes. Also, repeating a mantra can replace conscious or subconscious negativity—which could delay your beautiful creations. By chanting a mantra, you can protect your mind from karmic thoughts that have left impressions on your soul, consciousness, brain and body due to your past choices and actions. A mantra can replace negative self-talk with super sounds that will bring you the manifestation of your heart's desire.

As the ancient Rishis have taught, subtle sounds, or the mantras that you have internalized and aren't audible, become more powerful than gross sounds. Subtle sounds and even special syllables can reach deeper layers of your mind—and this is a powerful process, as 90 percent of your thinking is below your conscious awareness.

And most of this subconscious material is creating your current life. So without guidance and expanded awareness, you may never get to know the *actual* thoughts that are sabotaging your happiness. This is the reason why prolonged repetition of an auspicious mantra can change your negative (and repetitive) patterns that bring financial scarcity, a bad relationship, stress, or feelings of being unworthy of love, happiness, health and joy.

Affirmations

Affirmations, too, can raise your consciousness and replace habitual thinking patterns that might be delaying the fulfillment of your goals. Carrying universal messages of positivity and life-sustaining concepts, affirmations can work on the brain and bring about positive emotions and healing.

And although affirmations aren't as powerful in changing your destiny as mantras—being the latter based on super sounds heard by the yogis during their scouting of the cosmos. Yet affirmations can restore your positive thinking and remind that thoughts are simply choices based on your intention or habit. And it's always up to you what thoughts you choose. So, to experience the fulfilling life you want, you need to think life-enhancing thoughts.

Affirmations will go and hit your mind. They will change your thought patterns. It is a prayer to the mind to give up its own limitations, so that it can be unlimited.

—DR. PILLAI

Meditation

Did you know that some types of meditation can slow down physical aging? Other techniques can attract to you the right people at the right time. Some can bring you a financial windfall. This is why I strongly believe that spiritual solutions are always the most powerful.

Meditation is a great way to get in touch with your true self. It gives you a better capacity to focus, reach a higher state of awareness and enhance your creativity. It is with the help of these spiritual practices that I've been able to change my life for the better every time I'd reached a *plateau* and felt stuck.

Countless studies prove that meditation can:
- Reduce stress
- Improve your heart health
- Help you breathe better and oxygenate your blood
- Improve the quality of your sleep
- Help you lose weight
- Reverse aging
- Help you drop self-limiting beliefs
- Improve your immune system
- Give you a clear and focused mind
- Reduce high blood pressure
- Give you a sense of connectedness
- Eliminate a feeling of isolation

- Help you resist or discard useless thoughts
- Increase useful and creative thinking
- Discover your true self
- Supernormal powers

I swear to you, there are divine things more beautiful than words can tell.

—WALT WHITMAN

CHAPTER 9

The 12 Spiritual Laws of Success and Bliss

*When you do things from your soul you feel a river moving in you,
a joy.*

—RUMI

You don't need to know Vedic astrology to benefit from its wealth of knowledge. Just follow the easy steps in this book and you'll be empowered to reach your higher potential and your life purpose. Each of the 12 Spiritual Laws is based on an aspect of astrology called "House" or a sector of the zodiac that corresponds to an area of your life.

The *12 astrological houses* in your birth chart offer a *framework* to explain deep truths about your life. The bliss that you'll find in the spiritual laws and their universal truths will stem from your awareness as you uncover your unique and sacred role in this lifetime.

The following 12 spiritual principles along with the meditations and guidance will help you discover or deepen your inner gifts of intuition, love, nurturing, receptivity, and creativity to manifest a life you love.

Karma and Vedic astrology are interlinked subjects.

—DR. PILLAI

The biggest obstacle to reaching your goals and fulfilling your desires is your mindset or karma. Of course, some circumstances and people might seem to be external factors contributing to your dissatisfaction and delays. In reality, karma is the law of cause and effect that resides in your thoughts—springing from your conscious, subconscious, and unconscious mind, genetics, and environment. So we attract people and circumstances based on this law.

And it's through our thoughts that planets and other celestial bodies influence us and create our consciousness. You will soon be able to rewire your thinking for success, letting go of debilitating self-doubts.

Each Spiritual Law will come alive to fit your unique circumstances and needs. Everything on earth is subject to these 12 Spiritual Laws, not only humans but also events, animals and inanimate matter.

I've used these tools and knowledge to fix myriad issues that kept cropping up in my life and helped my family, clients and students. I wish that no one had to go through unnecessary challenges alone. Here you'll find a friend who understands you, who's experienced many of the same problems and found an easier way of solving them. I'm so excited that I can now share what I've learned, which has already helped thousands positively transform their lives.

Make your life a masterpiece; imagine no limitations on what you can be, have or do.

—BRIAN TRACY

Let your life lightly dance on the edges of time like dew on the tip of a leaf.

—RABINDRANATH TAGORE

FIRST SPIRITUAL LAW
You're Amazing

When you shine your authentic self, you become more attractive and successful. With your Source, you're the co-creator of your experiences. You have great inborn powers to accomplish anything you set out to achieve.

1st house

Self, Body, Life Path, Interests, True Self

Affirmation for Self-Empowerment

I'm an infinite being. I'm beautiful and every day I acquire the knowledge I need for a successful and blissful life. I am divine light in tridimensional form. I can do anything I set my mind on.

Planetary Ruler of the 1st House

The planet that rules the first house is the Sun.

In Vedic astrology, the 1st house—also known as *ascendant*—is the sign or constellation rising in the East on the horizon at the time of your birth. This house, its ruling planet and the archetypes that are connected with it create your main outlook on life, helping you set priorities and goals.

According to the yogis, you have both divine and royal origins. Achieving royalty consciousness is both a positive goal and your responsibility towards others, as royalty implies both service and self-sacrifice.

Even if we're self-centered, to be motivated by compassion is good because it leads to self-confidence, less fear and greater trust.

—DALAI LAMA

Also, the 1st house teaches you to like yourself. Your physical beauty, your general appearance and your inner beauty are one and the same, and will contribute to your success. In fact, the body is the garment your soul has chosen as a vehicle to gain more knowledge, and accomplish your goals in this life. According to the Rishis, we take many lives in order to acquire more knowledge. The 1st house shows your sense of self.

Don't let others dictate what will be attractive to you. Decide to like the physical you and declare it as worthy and attractive to you, thereby rejecting comparisons and opinions of others.

—WAYNE W. DYER

You Have Unlimited Potential

The first house has a great revelation for *you have unlimited capacities that have remained dormant.* The power of your soul is infinite and you're constantly evolving. Nothing happens by mistake and your soul is the movie director of your life.

Usually, we aren't aware of our higher potential. Too often, our educational system isn't equipped to teach us how to bring out the best in us.

On the contrary, the ancient Rishis were fully conscious and knew their potential. Often, they lived in hermitages in the forest and came out to teach the worthy and righteous.

Many Rishis just spent their lives in meditation—like the present yogis who live in seclusion—to gain a powerful consciousness and explore their inner powers.

To this goal, they used various techniques—special breathing exercises, meditations, visualizations and recitation of sound waves or mantras. Yet they didn't want power for the sake of it—but rather wished to rise above the limitations of their own physical bodies and minds and help humanity.

The first house teaches you to trust your intuition and intelligence— and develop an inner compass to be guided to the right knowledge for your unique life path.

Be Empowered by The Sun

The Sun is the natural ruler of the 1st house. The Sun is also the soul—which shows how your true self has chosen a path to evolution by taking a physical incarnation at this time.

The Sun teaches you that your vitality depends largely on your self-esteem.

This is also the belief of Ayurveda—our immune system works only when we love and respect ourselves. In other words, self-esteem keeps you healthy. Be the master of your life by taking care of your body through healthy exercise and your mind through beneficial meditation.

Then your path will be revealed to you: let the 'self' illuminate your life journey.

Moreover, the Sun indicates your authority figure— your father, your government officials and employer. A good 1st house with beneficial planetary placements shows that you will have good relationships with these individuals.

Perfect am I
Perfect is my mind,
Perfect are my eyes,
Perfect are my ears,
Perfect is my breath,
Perfect is my entire being,
At peace with myself am I.

—ATHARVA VEDA 19.51.1

Practice One or More of the Following Easy Meditations to Increase Your Self-Esteem and Your Wealth

---

To acquire royalty consciousness all that is needed is to change the light energy within your pituitary gland. Then you will think differently.

—DR. PILLAI

Meditation

Pituitary Gland or 3rd Eye

Throughout the day, put your attention on the forehead, in the middle of your eyebrows.

Even when you're busy talking to others, try to keep an awareness of this point.

This easy meditative technique will strengthen your intuition and you will rely on *self-referral*—increasing your self-trust. You will then receive accurate information about circumstances and other people and will be protected from lies or manipulation.

Your creativity will receive a boost and you'll be able to work faster and more efficiently. As an added bonus, you'll be guided to form healthier relationships with compatible people. This technique can also benefit all your activities.

Meditation

"Who Am I?"

Meditating on the question "Who Am I?" will work in subtle ways to change the perception of who you are. Your limited perspective of yourself will be enormously expanded. You'll feel infinite and divine.

In yoga philosophy, the question "Who am I?" is a good starting point for your spiritual transformation—which can ultimately take you to your highest potential and even spiritual enlightenment.

In India, there are two main traditions that use the question "Who Am I" as a tool for evolution. The first is for ascetic students of the so-called Vedanta, or the end of the Vedas.

The second is more helpful for the purpose of this book. It's the tradition that teaches the path of the Goddess—or Divine Feminine—which, according to the yogis and Rishis, can take you to the greatest happiness and bliss that are possible on this earth plane.

- Set a timer for 3 minutes.
- Close your eyes. Ask the question: "*Who Am I?*" Keep repeating the question and listen to your spontaneous answers without judgment.
- In the first week, it's ok to recite these sounds aloud.
- Later, try it mentally. If chanting mentally doesn't work for you, continue chanting out loud.

- No matter what answers come from your mind, vow to like yourself no matter what.

In time, you'll realize more and more that you're not just your profession, your social background, your bank account, your affiliations, or gender. Soon you'll see that you're an infinite being with infinite possibilities.

Meditation

Expansion of Your Consciousness
- Set a timer for 10 minutes.
- Sit comfortably and close your eyes. When you close your eyes, your intuition increases.
- Put your attention on your body. Feel your body. If you feel pain somewhere, put your attention on that body part first.
- Affirm "I have the power to create what I need and I am infinite."
- Feel love for yourself. If you cannot, remember a person who loves you. Feel that love.
- See yourself as a light being. Feel the immense power for being your true spiritual self.
- Visualize yourself as a beautiful Goddess or God. If you're not sure of how that looks, you can search online for an image that resonates with you.
- Relax. Slowly, open your eyes.

Real Life

In my mid-20s, I just had moved to Rome from Bergamo, in the north of Italy. Rome was my favorite city and I loved my work as a freelance journalist. But, sadly, I wasn't earning enough to cover my expenses. So I applied for a position as a real estate agent in a local firm that sold luxury condos.

During the first interview, I was pretty nervous—I knew nothing about real estate or that particular firm. During the interview, I suddenly blurted out, "You must hire me! I already have an apartment in Rome, so I don't have to relocate to work here. I can start right away."

My statement came as a total *non sequitur* to what was being asked. My words had made no sense to me and was sure that my interviewers thought the same. Even I was surprised at my statement.

As I drove home, I repeated mentally that sentence many times, internally rolling my eyes in regret. I eventually shrugged, and I was sure I didn't get the position.

The next day, one of the interviewers called me for another meeting. "Really?" I almost shouted, but managed to sound calm. As I entered her office, again I felt naïve and inexperienced for the way I had handled my first interview.

But she looked amused. "Never before we'd heard something like that during an interview." Confused, I asked for clarification. "It was bold and refreshing," and repeated my statement that they had to hire me because I already had a home in Rome.

"We had to give you the position," she said. "Your self-confidence was just what we need." And that is how I landed that job.

Though this episode might look like sheer luck, over the years I realized that others respond better to your ideas and desires when you are being authentic. Of course, there are boundaries no one should cross.

But in general, authenticity, trusting more, and worrying less about how others perceive you, might just add a special energy to your aura.

Dress and decorate yourself beautifully according to your taste and with the best clothes you can afford. There's a science behind this, too. Others will treat you differently, and being well dressed will even improve your cognitive functions, according to some studies.

Clothes have a tremendous power to affect your psychology, the psychology of onlookers and your fortune.

—DR. PILLAI

I believe that it's worth spending some time thinking about this. I grew up in Italy where I was taught about beauty—nature, arts, clothes and design. Because of this upbringing, I never felt that my appearance was a superficial aspect of my life.

Have you ever felt the pain of showing up underdressed to a party or social gathering? I have—and it's no fun. I now believe that it's better to overdress. Can you imagine a lovely Goddess or God from any tradition being dressed in rags? The way you present yourself is very important.

Love Yourself: Your Income Depends on It

The way you feel about yourself can determine your income. Think of someone who works in your same field and is earning ten times more money than you. As irritating this might seem, one of the reasons for the disparity is in the consciousness of that person who will not accept anything less.

So, position yourself for success. Always love yourself, yet always try to correct your negative traits without any self-loathing.

Purify your speech by speaking sweetly, speaking the truth, speaking carefully. Purify the eyes to be vigilant and have foresight.
—SHUKLA YAJUR VEDA

This passage of the Yajur Veda is believed to purify the character and karma of those who recite it and follow these guidelines. We should use positive and meaningful words. We should never use satire, bad, fraudulent or vulgar speech. Instead, we should sweetly speak the truth with a pure heart and soul.

Of course, we need to keep these basic tenets in mind:

- Being respectful
- Meaning no harm. Which doesn't mean you shouldn't take actions that others might dislike—rather, just check your motives and make sure you're being ethical.
- If you've been wronged, speak up, don't act up.
- Compliment others for their good qualities or work. Chances are they will reciprocate.
- Err on the side of politeness and respect.

O Radiant One! Inspire the diligent and the successful to earn wealth.
—RIG VEDA

SECOND SPIRITUAL LAW
Prosperity Is Your Divine Right

When you honor both your values and your desires, your efforts lead to financial good fortune. Settling for less than you truly appreciate doesn't honor your divine origins, nor does it benefit the world. When you embrace thoughts of abundance, the universe always supports you.

2ND HOUSE

Wealth, Assets, Family, Legacy, Values, Food, Mouth

Affirmation for Wealth

I now live my life according to my higher values. As a result, my financial wealth grows every day.

Planetary Ruler of the 2nd House

The planet that rules the second house is Jupiter, the planet of wisdom and wealth.

Parashara, one of the great sages who wrote about Vedic astrology, identified the second astrological house as the energy of wealth, the human face, the food you eat, your family, and your valuables, such as precious gems and assets. The planet associated with this house is generous Jupiter, the celestial body that rules expansion, higher wisdom, positivity, faith and wealth.

What do you *really* value and wish for? Is it money, a happy family life, precious jewelry, a collection of artworks? Try not to judge your desires—as long as they harm no one and you use ethical means, you have the God-given right to fulfill your desires.

If you want money, a good income, comforts and even luxury, allow yourself to receive them. God isn't poor—and despite common beliefs, God does not want you to be poor.

My teacher Dr. Pillai, a phenomenologist of religion and a Siddha yoga master calls himself a spiritual scientist. He recently gave a public interpretation of one of Jesus' teachings:

"Blessed be ye poor." He revealed that the Aramaic word 'blessed' in use during the time of Jesus actually meant "wealthy."

Apparently, Jesus blessed his devotees and wished them to become rich: "Ye poor people, may you be rich." His words were a technology to change the consciousness of the poor crowd to bring them material and spiritual wealth.

Ask me, and I will make the nations your inheritance, the ends of the earth your possession.

—PSALM 2:8

Sounds and Vibrations Can Make You Wealthy and Happy

God created the world through the Word. The Word is mantra.

—DR. PILLAI

The second house is also the house of speech. According to Vedic astrology and ancient yogic beliefs, we live in a vibratory universe. Scientists and theoretical physicists who are proponents of the "superstring theory" agree with this view that everything vibrates.

The Bible says that in the beginning of the creation of the cosmos there was the "word." The Rishis and yogis said that the primordial sound of creation was *AUM* or *OM*. This sound is said to be the secret of our vibratory universe.

According to *string theory,* vibrations reign in the universe—and both vibrations and sounds can influence our environment and even our health. Apparently, every object and celestial body in the universe is made of energy and vibrating filaments called "strings."

Even in Ayurveda, the ancient healing system of India, there's reference to the healing effects of sounds—in the so-called *Gandarva* music—or classical melodies with the power to harmonize both your external and inner environments.

Your thoughts are also sound and vibrating energy that can influence your life and the environment.

The ramifications of this tenet of the yogis are very important for your happiness. It is then paramount to think only thoughts that can manifest what you want. Sounds are also the traditional mantras used by the yogis to manifest and change their consciousness, and even more powerful are the names of divine beings—such as Shiva, Christ, Vishnu, Brahma, and Lakshmi, for example.

The Ancient Goddess of Sound

In the Rig Veda, the oldest of the Vedas, a Goddess named *Vaak*, meaning speech, was considered the mother of all sacred texts, as well as the muse of all poets and philosophers. She was said to be the mother of all languages on our planet and in the cosmos.

Goddess Vaak only spoke words that manifested the desired objects—so powerful was the force behind the syllables she uttered.

Every time you speak, you transmit information through an energy field using sound waves. There is information in the words you select, and the energy is the electromagnetic impulse that travels through cyberspace.

—DEEPAK CHOPRA

If you find it hard to identify and communicate your highest values, it may be difficult for you to create a beautiful life. So, awareness and clear communication of your needs and desires can help you manifest your cherished dreams.

The sounds in your thoughts and words work on different levels. To manifest your goals and acquire wealth, you need to watch your habitual language and inner dialogue. Your self-talk is equally important because your thoughts are the source of your experiences. Much of your inner conversation happens on the subconscious level.

Using powerfully positive language in the form of sacred mantras, names of God, and positive affirmations will help you create what you want to attract into your life.

Your words can be considered a karmic imprint, because every thought has an impact on your life—even the smallest sound can change your brain, decisions and outcomes. How? It's because thoughts are sounds, and sounds vibrate. So if you hold negative thoughts and your language is rife with negative expressions coming from the subconscious, it could be very difficult for you to succeed.

A positive sound, instead, becomes like the seed of a tree—you may not see the tree, but the tree will grow, because it's encoded in that tiny seed.

The Sounds in Your Language

I've always been fascinated by foreign and ancient languages, especially by how different people expressed themselves. I noticed that invariably their speech reflected their lives and vice versa. For example, the rich and famous speak with tons of positivity and creativity. I also noticed that poor people, in general, speak words of resignation, scarcity, fear and regret.

Of course, a person from France will hold certain beliefs that may be different from those of an African. And the saints I've met spoke words of wisdom and universal love.

So we need to stay alert and watch closely the words we choose to manifest what we want—letting in only positive and empowering thoughts.

Every time we transmit information via words, we communicate via an energy field that uses sound waves. Even if you send an email, you use information and energy. There are energy and information in the words you select. So, to make sure you select the best possible words, below I will show you what kind of speech will help for your manifestations.

Thinking can create. Thinking is sounds and sounds can create. Sounds bring intelligence.

—DR. PILLAI

MANTRA for the Goddess of Wealth

Devi Lakshmi rules over both outer and inner abundance, filling our lives with divine grace, bliss and beauty. Mantras for Goddess Lakshmi are very auspicious.

—YOGINI SHAMBHAVI

A powerful set of sounds or mantra for wealth that was revealed by Dr. Pillai is *SHREEM BRZEE.*

The sound Shreem Brzee works like a seed. You don't see the tree in the seed. The same way, Shreem Brzee has the total wealth of the universe embedded within it. All that you have to do is just say the sound over and over again.

—DR. PILLAI

Meditation for Wealth Creation

- MANTRA FOR WEALTH: SHREEM BRZEE
- Repeat it at least 108 times daily. Set a time in the day, preferably early morning to create a positive outlook throughout the day and attract wealth.
- You can also recite Shreem Brzee every day for 30 minutes to empower your mind for wealth manifestations.

Testimonials have shown that many people have manifested amazing money miracles—mansions, large and profitable businesses, and more.

Below are some easy ways to increase your awareness and help you select the best and most effective words for manifestation.

- Pay attention to the meaning of the sounds you use and whether they're really serving you. Beware of hidden negative meanings. Beware of slang and colloquialisms that are rife with negativity.
- At first, expressions like "kick ass" or "kick start" seem harmless and affirmative. And if you look deeper, you may find that your body and mind become tense when you read or use these words. They tell of a 'rat race' and reveal their inherent aggressiveness, yet lack true power.
- Even more at risk of using weak language are the younger generations, that are absorbing negative, violent entertainment. Many young individuals imitate their peers' weak expressions that are supposed to convey amazement and approval. Common are "That's insane" or "That's sick" to mean good or exceptional.
- But is this language really helpful when you want to tap into your divine creativity? Will it assist you in your amazing creations so you can reveal your hidden potential to the world? Probably not. Would you use cussing in an interview or at your son's

graduation? Then why use it in other circles? The yogis said that every word counts.

- I suggest affirmations like "I'm the winner." Or you can congratulate yourself and others on a regular basis after even a small achievement.
- Better yet, compassion awakens our higher intelligence. So, visualize people who suffer for lack of food and water. For a moment feel their pain. Send to the universe a wish that everyone gets sufficient food, water, clothes and a good, safe home. Vow to do something to alleviate suffering on the planet—and voilà, you have now entered a realm of higher intelligence.
- Now affirm your willingness to tap into the field of higher creativity and infinite possibilities to create the beautiful life of your dreams.
- Repeat often, "I will win." Or "I let go of all my hesitation and fear, so I overcome any obstacle and win." Or "I now embrace my victory." These affirmations can help you acquire a positive mindset and you'll be more likely to create what you want.

Shreem Brzee is not an attempt nor effort that you will make or a tool that you will use just to make money. This sound itself is life. The sound itself is wealth.

—DR. PILLAI

- The Vedas were written in a poetic form because verses can convey powerful meanings without the obstacles of our everyday language from the rational mind. These were most powerful affirmations in the form of poems, which were infused with incredible beauty and positivity. If these verses are too complex for you to read or memorize, you can use common mantras— like *OM* or *Shreem*, as these sounds originated in the cosmos and were pulled down by the yogis.
- Even subconscious thoughts create—so it's very important to dig deeper and understand your thought patterns about wealth, health, relationships, and happiness.

- Be aware of your beliefs, too. For example, if your hidden belief is, *"Rich people are corrupt."* Or if you grew up hearing *"There's never enough money,"* you might have internalized this belief and it's now influencing your level of income. Change your beliefs according to your dreams and goals. Avoid the common expression *"filthy rich."* Although it seems harmless, it conjures negative imagery that might subconsciously stop you from creating what you want.
- Practice reciting the mantra *Shreem Brzee* as often as you can and especially late at night—when others are sleeping and their consciousness doesn't influence you. You might get more clarity and revelations and the effects are more powerful. Then after creating what you want, it will be easier to share with others your good fortune or discoveries into the realm of consciousness, which is infinite and amazing.
- Mantras can put a shield of protection around you and change your mindset from scarcity to abundance. You might even feel that wealth and abundance are already yours. This new mindset is a powerful mechanism and will bring you new ideas for wealth creation.

Mantras are power sounds discovered by yogis in their deep meditation. They pulled the mantras from space. Space, ether is full of the intelligence of the highest kind.

—DR. PILLAI

Real Life

Have you ever had the experience of hearing a foreign language that sounds melodious and pleasant to you? Or have you felt that another language could arouse tension and even fear in you? I believe there are karmic reasons for our likes and dislikes for some languages.

The theory of rebirth or reincarnation makes so much sense in this case, especially when we look at the many studies and the extensive research in this field.

At university, I studied literature and languages. Because I was really passionate about these subjects, I spent most of my free time reading extracurricular English and French classics, magazines, newspapers— even though they weren't required by my professors.

I especially loved learning *glottology*—the study of the roots of each word, which showed both their cultural origins and hidden meanings.

Since I was 5 years old and took my first class in English, I had a deep love for this language. In high school, I excelled in Latin and failed classical Greek—a language I truly disliked. In my second college year, I added to my courses an ambitious goal: the study of German literature and language.

Although some of my Italian friends had shared horror stories about their boarding school in Germany and tried to dissuade me, I loved the German culture: even its difficult grammar, the impenetrable philosophy and classics. I signed up and after some time I really enjoyed my studies.

Fast-forward to my mid-thirties after getting married and moving to the U.S.

While I was deeply immersed in my morning meditation, I saw myself in another life in an Italian city where I've never lived before, and in a time in history many years before I was born.

For some mysterious reason, I'd always disliked that beautiful part of Italy, and even felt uneasy when I heard the accent of those who lived there.

Within a few seconds, I saw an entire lifetime. I was a woman, but I looked different—even though I knew beyond any doubt that this woman and I were the same person.

After less than a minute, I opened my eyes and realized that many of the current circumstances in my life were due to that previous life. This experience also revealed the reasons for my likes and dislikes, and my love for German culture.

It also explained the challenges that I was undergoing in this life, the reasons behind the people I chose in my current life, and the blessings within the lessons I had learned.

Your Soul Uses Symbols Instead of Words

Each power symbol—an animal seen in a dream, a God or Goddess you read about, a crystal, a gem—can be powerful ways of connecting with the language of your soul. This language has the power to transform you.

Take for example the Indian Goddess Lakshmi. Notice the jar overflowing with gold coins in her hands, and the two lovely white elephants at each side. You might not know anything about this Goddess—but your subconscious will immediately identify the archetype of immense wealth, beauty, and luxury.

- Surround yourself with images and symbols of what you want to manifest. Choose real gold coins or images of jewels if you want a bigger paycheck or a multimillion-dollar business that allows you to buy a yacht or a luxury car.
- Maybe you want an image of a lovely home filled with lush green plants. Add colorful paintings on the walls—and so on, according to your taste.
- Be specific, for example: A luxury lounge chair in pure white. Find an image online or magazine that resembles your ideal chair.

Your beliefs become your thoughts. Your thoughts become your words. Your words become your actions. Your actions become your habits. Your habits become your values. Your values become your destiny.
—MAHATMA GANDHI

Affirmation for Wealth

"I deserve rest, leisure and wealth. I'm rich and I can allow myself time off from work without feeling guilty. I'm very wealthy and my abundance makes me, my family, and the world happy."

Repeat it daily 3 consecutive times. You can also repeat it or paraphrase it to acquire new beliefs for your wealth manifestations.

5-Minute Meditation

- Set a timer and close your eyes.
- Visualize yourself swimming in a pool of gold coins. Notice the beauty of the shining gold—the metal of choice of the ancient gods, because of its purity and high vibrations. Feel the pleasure.
- Visualize a luxury object you've been dreaming about—a car, a necklace, a perfect precious ring. Not big on luxury? Visualize an ideal trip to a faraway country that you've been wanting to visit. See yourself packing, feel the fun and lightheartedness. At your arrival, see the beautiful décor in the comfortable hotel. See yourself sitting with an ideal companion under the stars (if it appeals to you) and feel the pleasant breeze and scent of flowers.
- Now relax and open your eyes.

Meditation on Gratitude

- Set a timer for 3 minutes.
- Write down three reasons you're grateful. This simple habit will lastingly reshape your thoughts and you'll start seeing positive changes in your life.

There's substantial scientific research on the power of gratitude. For example, a Harvard researcher and author Shawn Achor said: *"Something as simple as writing down three things you're grateful for every day for 21 days in a row significantly increases your level of optimism, and it holds for the next six months. The research is amazing."*

You may want to try for yourself to take control of your mindset and repetitive, negative thought patterns.

Successful people all have one thing in common: unbelievable drive. And the drive is not for money. The money is the by-product of what they do.

—LARRY KING

THIRD SPIRITUAL LAW
You're a Spiritual Warrior

When you take courageous action, passionately working on your goals, you step into a zone of strength and victory. Then your powerful desires will easily manifest your wishes.

3RD HOUSE

Will, Desire, Competition, Siblings, Peers, Classmates, Courage, Shoulders, Arms and Hands

---

Those who restrain their desires, do so because theirs is weak enough to be restrained.

—WILLIAM BLAKE

Affirmation

Every day I happily create what I want. I have abundant courage to face the competition and use my inner talents to defeat lethargy. I enjoy challenging myself to become better and better. I easily defeat my fears and succeed in my work and goals.

Planetary Ruler of the 3rd House: Mars

- Intentions leading to action
- Victory in competitions
- Competing with yourself
- Courageously improving your performance
- Being unafraid of competition

Action is the foundational key to all success.

—PABLO PICASSO

Your Desire is Your Fuel

The third house is called a *kama or desire house*. It reveals your efforts and courage to stand up for yourself when needed. This house also represents your peers, siblings and the way you communicate with the world.

This house of desire—and its emotional nature—is ruled by Mars, the planet of strength, energy, courage and competitive spirit. This planet is very beneficial for the arenas of the third house. In fact, we need a good amount of 'guts' to succeed in life—as we need to defend our principles from naysayers and even competitors.

Can you imagine if you had a small startup, and after investing most of your time and money, you just wanted to run away, and close shop because you're afraid of the competition? Or you launch a marketing campaign and instead of refining your skills, you start comparing yourself with your peers? Obviously, you would meet with failure.

So Mars can give you the stamina, strength and determination to succeed, or you would miss an opportunity, and delay reaching your goals.

The Courage to Take Action at the Right Time

Mars demands timely action to implement your successful ideas, because just contemplating your idea won't bring you wealth or success.

Similarly, at work you need to be strong—yet ethical—to get your work done and win the daily battles against lethargy or worse, forgetting your goals altogether.

You might have already experienced this—and had to confront an unacceptable situation at work. Although you might have been reluctant, you found the courage and faced that person or situation to right a wrong, or were able to prevent a negative outcome.

Sometimes action, however, requires the courage to leave a place and let go. So changing your job or profession are also powerful steps you can take to obtain a better lifestyle, more time with a loved one, or finally visiting France—which you've been dreaming to do since your college years.

Don't be bamboozled by the hypnosis of social conditioning.
—DEEPAK CHOPRA

Courage takes many forms—in fact, it's a shapeshifter—one day courage means dropping your ego and controlling your tongue. Another time, courage allows you to quit a cushy job with a nice paycheck—as I did—to end your suffering and restore your peace of mind and self-respect.

This gutsy move will lead you to find the perfect field where you can finally display your gifts and creativity, and even work with a more suitable team.

Courage is a love affair with the unknown.

—OSHO

So, if needed, be strong and distance yourself from a toxic place or peer. Save your energy to acquire new skills and win over your fears—most of all, work on yourself. In fact, the worst enemy is often found within, and working on yourself instead of battling with others is a sure path to success and peace of mind.

Courage, most importantly, means taking a leap of faith and leaving behind what isn't serving your purpose in life.

Of course, courage, actions and assertiveness need not be aggressive or dismissive of others. In fact, when you resist fears, you strive for excellence and become unlimited and boundless. Then your voice will be authentic and you'll stand out in a crowd.

Fearlessness is the first requisite of spirituality. Cowards can never be moral.

—MAHATMA GANDHI

Real Life

Sometimes, making changes isn't for the faint of heart. Can you imagine Steve Jobs or Mark Zuckerberg doing everything their fathers or mothers did? Thinking like their peers or siblings? Most innovation, in fact, requires great courage and a strong desire to make your mark. The two tech giants knew this and not only did they ignore previously explored paths, but they even turned to a spiritual Guru and his teachings to acquire the necessary inner strength to implement their Apple and Facebook ideas.

If your work requires writing and communication—as most jobs do—then the third house energy is one of the most important houses for you. Being firm and standing your ground is a must to resist skepticism—a natural default mechanism.

Have Clear Goals and Flex Your Muscles

Everything in the universe is energy. To give energy to your goals and manifest them you need plenty of focused attention and refined intention.

This is easier said than done, so below I show you how to keep your intentions strong so you can manifest them.

The will to win, the desire to succeed, the urge to reach your higher potential—these are keys to unlock your full potential.

—CONFUCIUS

Have you ever listed your daily goals in the morning, only to feel frustrated at night, when one mere item got checked while the remaining five just didn't happen? Here's where meditation becomes your best tool.

Meditation is not a method to simply calm the mind—as calmness is just a byproduct of meditation. What meditation really does is energize you, empower your brain and help you manifest your goals. This is something that sleep alone cannot do.

Meditation

- In the morning, as soon as you wake up, ask yourself, *"What do I really, really want?"* The first thought that comes to mind—that is the key to your manifestation.
- After uncovering your authentic desire, write it down 108 times in positive words. For example, write *"I want a wonderful new job."* And not, *"I don't want to work for XYZ."* Or write, *"I want to express myself authentically."* Not, *"I don't want to feel suppressed."*

Meditation

This meditation stops restless and unnecessary thoughts.

- Every day, take time out from your schedule to sit in a quiet place and close your eyes.
- Put your attention on your nostrils. Keep your attention on the nostrils even when thoughts come. Gently return to the nostrils each time.
- Remember, try not to struggle with the mind, avoid fighting with the mind. Be gentle.
- Ask for what you want. Trust that you'll get it.

Ask and what you asked will be given to you; seek and you will find; knock at a door and the door will be opened to you.

—MATTHEW 7:7

Practicing this for 10 minutes every day can help you experience new silence and peace—which naturally lead to more mental clarity to manifest your wishes. Meditation also reduces stress from excessive drive. Also, the ensuing mental peace can rejuvenate you on all levels.

Also, remember that faith *"the size of a mustard seed can move mountains."* Have faith in yourself and the Divine and you will experience miracles.

You can only get so far on human effort. Sometimes we need a little help from the Gods and then magic happens.

—KATHY GIBSON

Real Life

I'd chosen to work in public relations because I loved writing and the idea of promoting and connecting people I believed in. In fact, every time I helped my clients succeed, I was as happy as if I'd achieved the same for myself.

After a successful career helping entrepreneurs expand their business, grow restaurant chains, and get TV and print coverage, suddenly everything seemed to be falling apart.

I felt sluggish and began resenting my work. What I did even felt inauthentic and I became pessimistic. This was clearly a sign that I needed more meaning and purpose. But I ignored the signs.

At the office, I often felt bored and depressed. One day, I found myself watching traffic for hours from my office window, just waiting for the time to go home. Where had my enthusiasm gone? After that day, nothing was ever the same.

I also felt I was failing in my two new accounts—the first was a well-known institute of psychoanalysis that provided therapy to patients. After just one meeting with the director, I realized that they disliked my philosophy and Carl Jung, whom I loved.

The second client was a poet: a gifted elderly lady who wanted more recognition and visibility for her work.

I felt incredible stress and dreaded pitching media people about these two accounts. To be honest, I didn't really believe in their work and felt non-stop guilt for being unable to motivate myself and be helpful.

On the one hand, I preferred meditation to therapy. Meditation had worked wonders for me, especially after moving to the U.S., getting married, and giving birth to my first child. Back then, I was a 20-something in a new country, with no friends or family members.

On the other hand, my most difficult task was to publicize the books and poetry of the poet client, whose writing style I didn't enjoy. This was probably my fault, as I'd become hard to please due to my long years as a literature major.

Before taking on those accounts, I was being quoted in print and digital media, and influencers would ask me for new stories. I was thrilled.

Now, I felt I was letting down my clients, my boss, and myself. I couldn't stand the sense of failure, and I knew that my clients deserved better. So I asked my team for help and I doubled my efforts. I contacted all our most influential friends in the media. Results: nil.

To relieve the growing guilt, fear, and stress, I practiced yoga and meditation every morning before going to work.

On a particularly grueling day at the office, my glance fell on a line of a New York Times article: "I worked in PR and I was so stressed that I took up yoga. Then I liked yoga so much that I decided to quit my job to become a full-time yoga teacher."

I reread those lines over and over. This woman was so much like me—I wished I could do the same. Her story was my story. I was stunned that someone else from my professional background had developed my same passion for yoga. But—unlike me—she'd found the courage to quit her stressful job, and become a full-time yoga teacher. I so wished to do the same.

I no longer believe in coincidence, and I now know that those failing accounts were the results of my soul taking steps towards a new direction—one that would change my life for the better, and beyond my wildest dreams.

About a year later—and I regret that it took me a whole year to make that decision—I quit my PR position and enrolled in a yoga teacher certification program. Two years later, after more studies of yoga therapy, meditation, yoga philosophy—while enjoying every minute of it—I got my certificates and began teaching.

I wore yoga pants and sat cross-legged on the floor for up to 10 hours a day. I taught group classes and, I also had the opportunity to teach privately to some medical doctors, and others in the healing professions.

My clients were happy with the results, especially my private students who had my undivided attention and guidance. I felt incredibly fulfilled knowing that I was contributing to others' well-being and happiness.

Additionally, I felt great and healthier than ever before. I experienced a shift in consciousness and became more interested in service to humanity. My love and compassion for the poorest people on this planet also grew exponentially.

Meditation

Visualize your greatest three wishes. Try to muster as many positive emotions as you can during your visualizations.

Write your wishes down. Spend at least 15 minutes a day to write, read and daydream about them.

You were born to win. But to be a winner, you must plan to win, prepare to win, and expect to win.

—ZIG ZIGLAR

FOURTH SPIRITUAL LAW
You Are Love

When you protect yourself and others with the same love and selflessness that a mother shows to her child, your peace will be sublime. These same feelings will create a safe haven for you, true happiness and a home where you feel peaceful.

Moon, Mother, Home, Motherland, Unconditional Love, Happiness, Vehicles, Peace of Mind

And now my friends, all that is true, all that is noble, all that is just and pure, all that is loveable and gracious, whatever is excellent and admirable— fill all your thoughts with these things.

—PHILIPPIANS 4:8

Affirmation

I'm always peaceful and safe everywhere. I easily find ways to love and nurture myself and my loved ones. I feel loved and protected.

Planetary Ruler of the 4th House

The planet of the 4th house is the Moon.

The Moon represents the mind, its fluctuations, emotions and feelings. The Moon is considered one of the nine Vedic planets, and not a mere satellite. The Moon brings you intuition and unconditional love—a love that never ends and doesn't require to be reciprocal, like a mother's love for her child.

You've probably experienced a peaceful state of mind that led to deeply loving emotions. To feel love, we need peace. So thinking peaceful and loving thoughts helps you experience positive emotions.

"Before you think a thought, you should think if it's worth thinking that thought. If you practice this conscious thinking, you'll realize that most of the thoughts that come to you are indeed junky thoughts."

—DR. PILLAI

You have the choice to focus only on thoughts that bring you happiness, true love, security, and joy. Smiling can also power up your affirmations and shift your mood to a positive state.

Researcher and author Sondra Barrett has written *Secrets of Your Cells*, a book on the surprising effects of smiling. In her study, she found that smiling could defuse stress, increase productivity and improve cognitive abilities. More importantly, smiling could speed patients' healing of cancer.

The Mother

You must have noticed mothers' bright smiles when they look at their babies and small children. Mothers seldom hold back their love—and seem wired to keep giving more and more love and assistance to their offspring. Invariably, mothers are filled with emotions of empathy and tears of joy when they first glance at their infants after childbirth.

On this Earth do I stand,
Unvanquished, un-slain, unhurt.
Set me, O Earth, within the nourishing strength
That emanates from your body.
The Earth is my mother,
Her child I am.

—ATHARVA VEDA

Did you know that Yale's most popular class ever taught happiness? Obviously, the reason for this is that the human pursuit of happiness is a never-ending quest—unless we find peace and love within ourselves and in our environment. Your home, your closest loved ones, the peace and security you acquire from your education are all fourth house themes.

A primary symbol of the fourth house is the mother figure. She was the first person protecting and loving you. And much of what makes us secure adults stems from the caring and nourishment we received from our mothers while growing up.

If you were among those who didn't grow up with your birth mother, another person might have taken on that role to ensure your survival and well-being, becoming a source of support and nourishment to you as a baby and in childhood.

What knowledge and wisdom did your mother pass on to you? Honoring those lessons can empower you and allow you to nurture and love others in turn.

Sadly, many couldn't receive enough or any motherly love. In this case, honoring the Divine Feminine in all women or another mother figure can bring us similar beneficial effects—and the brain and emotions are positively changed by images of benevolent feminine archetypes and celestial beings.

Often a feeling that we were not loved or not lovable can impair our capacity to love and feel compassion. Needless to say, empathy can improve your relationships and vanquish a feeling of separation.

My mother was always a source of inspiration, if not support, because at times we were separated by unforeseeable events. Yet we always remained connected.

My Mom's Memory

Recently, my mother told me something about my first few years of life that I didn't know. When I was about two years old, she struggled to feed me at meal times. In my first three years, although I was healthy, I was seldom hungry. Apparently, I would only eat fruit—and refused to accept anything else. As a drink, I'd only have freshly squeezed orange juice—not milk.

I was happy that she shared this memory, which I took as an early sign of my future vegetarianism.

Honoring Your Mother Brings You Incredible Blessings

You don't need to agree with your mother to be devoted to her. Something as simple as shared memories can be a great enrichment to your life.

According to Vedic astrology, the love and respect you give your mother—even when you think that she doesn't deserve it—has profound ramifications on your psychology and leads to your good fortune. In fact, in the Vedic tradition being respectful and devoted to our mothers is said to bring us the highest blessings.

In India, there's a saying that if a son is wealthy and successful, his mother must have loved him very much. The great Indian sages or Rishis knew the importance of honoring one's mother, calling it one of our most important duties in life.

According to the yogis, if your mother is no longer with you, honoring the Divine Feminine, other women, and especially other mothers can have a healing and positive effect on your spiritual evolution, and even your finances.

In fact, they believed that receiving the blessings from one's mother was the most important prerequisite for success in life. Moreover, in the Vedic tradition, the mother is honored like a Goddess.

Steps to Success and Bliss

Love is the highest vibration. Allow yourself to receive love unconditionally from others. Give love from your heart unconditionally to yourself and others. You will experience the highest state of consciousness possible.

—SRI SRI RAVI SHANKAR

Step 1: Connect with Peace and Love

- Becoming like a mother to yourself and others—by caring and supporting—can bring you more peace, a sense of connection and safety that can foster your projects and goals alike.

Step 2: Create a Safe Haven

- Make your home a loving abode for yourself and loved ones. Meditation can help you create peace in your heart, so you radiate peace in your home and extend your love to all. If you like the scent of sweet incense, you can try burning a stick and experience a change of consciousness. You might like its calming effects. Similarly, essential oils with a sweet scent of rose, jasmine or sandalwood are traditional Ayurveda remedies to remove stress and enhance your mood.

Step 3: Discover and Nurture Yourself

- Select one or two archetypes—a mythical being or real person whose qualities are so powerfully attractive that you could easily solve all your problems if you owned some of their traits.
- Try to choose an archetype with qualities of kindness, compassion, strength, and super intelligence. Images of Gods and Goddesses can help you to expect positive outcomes in your activities and relationships.
- Find some clothes or objects that remind you of this beautiful and powerful being. You'll see that putting your thoughts on this archetype can vanquish your self-doubt and increase your capacity to receive love, wealth, happiness and peace into your life. Spend a few minutes a day to meditate on this being.

Time invested in meditation is investing in mastering both matter and spirit.

—DR. BASKARAN PILLAI

Step 4: Be Centered in Your Heart

- Allowing yourself to feel unconditional love, compassion and protective feelings, and cultivating these qualities through meditation, journaling or simply awareness can increase your happiness.

Presently, the eyes, the ears, and all the senses delude us. We have to get beyond the senses to access full consciousness and bliss.

—DR. BASKARAN PILLAI

The Goddess

The Goddess energy is present in all mothers and mother figures. She is still worshipped in India. She has temples you can go to and connect with Her.

In Vedic literature, the celestial feminine energy is the most powerful—because everything we want in life comes through the Goddess energy of beautiful creation.

So beauty, joy, luxury, nurturing, protection, and love can come to you via the Divine Feminine. In our modern world filled with robotics and gadgets, surrounding yourself with life-enhancing images of a Goddess from any spiritual tradition can improve your mood, and bring more power and loveliness into your living space. You will then be able to absorb her delightful energy into your consciousness. Remember—where you put your attention that is where your energy goes.

In order to put an end to your suffering, you have to go and seek out the divine Source, the Goddess.

—DR. PILLAI

Try this:

Choose a gentle, nurturing Goddess—because Durga or Kali, for example, are warrior archetypes that can give you a sense of security, yet cannot foster the gentleness and flow you need to tap into your creativity.

The Goddess is ready to give us a wonderful opportunity for full consciousness. Once you taste the full consciousness and intelligence that she gives you, you'll understand how easy it is to live your life.

—DR. PILLAI

Perfect examples of lovely archetypes are the Goddesses that rule the Moon— Parvati and Lalitha Tripura Sundari. These are different names of the Divine Mother. She's pure energy and absolute beauty and can bring you love, purity of thoughts, and bliss.

We are born of love. Love is our mother.

—RUMI

Meditation

- Set a timer for 10 minutes. Gently close your eyes.
- Put your attention on your nostrils.
- Do it again every time that the mind wanders.
- Now move your attention to the heart. Connect with your emotional heart by putting your attention on the center of your chest.
- Relax more deeply by visualizing the love in your heart as a golden light.
- Let your mind and energy shift with the help of this golden light. Feel the light.
- Smile softly.
- When you're ready, slowly open your eyes.

When you repeat these steps before a meeting, or just prior to leaving your home in the morning, you'll notice that you feel more creative and confident.

Others, too, will see you differently—maybe they'll perceive you as more efficient or just as a nicer and more attractive person. They might even go out of their way to help you.

Gardeners are good at nurturing, and they have a great quality of patience. They're tender. They have to be persistent.

—RALPH FIENNES

A group meditation early in the morning is also a fabulous way to create peace and trust in your workplace and with your colleagues. Even CEOs are now adding meditation rooms to their work space for themselves and their employees. They know that productivity increases when we're happy, calm and in a more creative state—rather than anguished from overwork and fear.

Patiently, you can develop your practice and nurture it every day. Your positive and loving thoughts will blossom out of your daily practice. Your outlook will bring you joy and equally positive people.

You can also empower your dreams and goals with love. So envelop your goals with your love and joy. This will go a long way to manifesting them.

Power of Daydreaming

Daydream and enjoy your dreams in your mind—as Dr. Pillai teaches, you need to conceive something before you can manifest it. When you imagine, your midbrain has no idea that it's only make-believe. The brain will be flooded with happiness and you'll be empowered to create what you want.

If you don't choose to be happy, no one can make you happy. Don't blame God for that. And if you choose to be happy, no one can make you unhappy.

—PARAMAHANSA YOGANANDA

An Easy Shift to Bliss

Not the ones speaking the same language, but the ones sharing the same feeling understand each other.

—RUMI

Guard your mind and senses from unnecessary noise, and especially shocking images or controversial entertainment. These Ayurveda guidelines for longevity and perfect health can also protect your consciousness from unwanted, negative thought forms.

The fluid, watery and emotional nature of the fourth house makes for a highly sensitive environment—yet if you create a beautiful, peaceful space where you feel *at home* and *at peace,* this environment can provide you with the love, bliss and support you need for yourself and your loved ones.

Love is everything we need. "Love is God," says my teacher Dr. Pillai. For these reasons doing what you love, maintaining a secure place in which you feel loved and nurtured are keys to success and long-term happiness.

Try to surround yourself with loving and supportive people who care about you and your happiness. If you don't have this love and support in your life now, you might need to make some firm decisions to create a more nurturing environment and bring loving people into your life. A strong intention can be compared to powerful fuel that can rearrange both your subconscious thoughts to fit your goals, and can even shape your environment to let the universe accommodate your intention.

Spiritual counseling gives the ultimate solution.

—DR. PILLAI

Meditation

- Set a timer for 5 minutes. Sit in a quiet place.
- Close your eyes. (You can also play soft music of a healing frequency—search to find one suitable for your taste.)
- Put your attention on your nostrils. Notice how your thoughts immediately slow down.
- Every time a thought comes, gently put your attention on your nostrils.
- Now, remember a time when you felt totally loved and accepted. Hold that feeling. Visualize it. Enjoy it. What does it feel like it? Is it peaceful? Joyful? Is there a light in it? Was it nighttime?
- Can't remember any special time when you felt truly loved? Then imagine being in love. What does it feel like? Is it a gentle feeling? Is there acceptance? Hold on the images of your ideal state of love and bliss. Maybe it's a sunset, a place of worship, a flower garden, a cozy room decorated in pastel colors or natural whites. It's your choice.
- Relax.

Real Life

House of Vehicles:

I remember the day I saw it: it was white and silver, shiny, new, and had delicate cream-colored interiors. It looked beautiful. It was a Land Rover Discovery.

At that time, I was driving a forest-green Jeep that had become too *well-worn* by driving my children daily to their sports practices with my dog Chip, food shopping, and for family outings.

I loved this new white car's pristine appearance. It made me happy even to just look at it. It was out of my reach.

Then after talking with my husband, describing the car, its spaciousness and comforts, it turned out that we could afford it. So we went ahead and signed the papers.

I drove it home and my husband followed me in his car. I never let anyone else drive it. I finally could understand some people's love for their vehicles—which had made no sense to me before.

That was by far my favorite car—and probably the one my children, my dog and I enjoyed the most.

Being the fourth house the astrological sector of vehicles, this is one of the ways its energy and happiness manifests in your life through the acquisition of a lovely car, bicycle, scooter, plane, boat, and more.

FIFTH SPIRITUAL LAW
You Have Divine Knowledge

When you use your inborn divine intelligence, and educate yourself to create only the very best, your projects and creations will be outstanding. And the divine creativity hidden both in you and the cosmos will flow into everything you do. This higher intelligence brings you honors, success and wealth. Your life flourishes.

5TH HOUSE

Previous Lives, Intelligence, Creativity, Mantras, Wealth, Romance, Divine Knowledge, Children

What keeps life fascinating is the constant creativity of our soul.
—DEEPAK CHOPRA

Affirmation

I express the intelligence of the Divine at every moment. My life is filled with unending abundance and lovely creations. I learn and I create through the powers of my soul.

Planetary Ruler of the 5th House

The Planet of the fifth house is Jupiter.

Love is life. Love is intelligence. Love is creation. Love is God.
——DR. PILLAI

The fifth house teaches us that romance, intelligence, pure knowledge and creativity are divine forces that move the cosmos.

Jupiter, the planet of faith, children, wealth and optimism is the natural ruler of this house. Your creativity and wealth are divine gifts that come to you from your past spiritual merits and good deeds.

Jupiter is the source of higher beliefs and infinite positivity—these alone have the power to defeat disbelief, skepticism and fear that separate us from our divine potential.

If you believe it, you will have it.
——DR. PILLAI

Whether it's the creation of another being, as in giving birth to a child, or the expression of your artistic and creative self, something awesome and divine is at work.

Vedic astrology teaches that turning to your Source for guidance, following a righteous path, finding beauty in romance and serving others—all lead to greater happiness.

Jupiter's legendary generosity will reward you in unimaginable ways. So more intelligence, wisdom, wealth and happiness will easily come to you.

Divine intelligence is both within and without. In fact, by having divine origins you can have the life you want—you have all the powers within.

Believing in angelic and celestial beings, as Vedic astrology teaches, can enhance your life and is said to bring you miracles.

The Goddess or Divine Feminine brings to the earth plane all loveliness and wealth. The Rig Veda says that the Goddess is an embodiment of love, intelligence, motherly protection, and power. Mantras or traditional sounds that chant her name are believed to manifest your wishes faster than chanting names of male Gods.

In general, what creates is the sound, because sound is intelligence. Intelligence is just a sound wave that is able to open the brain and enables you to conceive. Only when you conceive you can deliver.

—DR. PILLAI

When your work and creative projects embody love—your self-confidence will grow, you'll become more powerful and know the field of infinite possibilities. Your creativity will be boundless, too.

A creative person knows nothing of problems. To choose a lifestyle that is not creative is to remain miserable. Only creators know what joy is.

—OSHO

In Vedic astrology, the fifth house is also considered one of the three main houses of education. So to be successful, you need to remain open to divine guidance and be willing to acquire new knowledge. This will help you reach all your goals.

Your hidden and very powerful potential will unfold through faith and trust. Then not even the sky will be the limit for your creations.

When we say no to a sad or mediocre life that makes us feel inadequate, unfulfilled and unloved, we can have a clean slate. Only when we realize that we are not alone, we can turn to the divine in full trust and surrender. Then a miracle happens—you'll be able to tap into the blissful nature of your soul.

From your soul will spring endless creativity and the happiness to be just you—a perfect expression of the divine waiting to blossom. It is your birthright to live an exclusive life filled with extraordinary experiences, because God is neither poor nor bored.

This is the promise of the fifth house—and your divine knowledge will take you to your infinite potential, opening to you the source of love, bringing you greater self-worth and revealing to you your authentic, divine nature. You were not meant to struggle. Rather, you are the receiver of all that God has to offer.

Service: Power Tool for Success

The Goddess is not simply a vibration or frequency. She is a mega-divine female, the mother-divine. As the counterpart of God, the Father, she is the Creatress of the phenomenal world.

—DR. PILLAI

Real Life

Even the smallest effort can make a difference when you're motivated by helping others.

Because I was passionate about Yoga Nidra, the yogic deep relaxation technique that I described earlier, I decided to offer free each day 30 minutes for those who wanted to experience it.

So I wrote a flyer explaining the benefits of this practice and selected a later time slot: 7:30 p.m.–8 p.m. Although this wasn't a popular time at the health club where I taught, and just a few members came after work, this became a very popular class.

In fact, it was one of my most successful teachings—many stressed teenagers and adults showed up to take my class. I particularly remember two girls who told me that during final exams, they would study and never leave their home, but they eagerly went out at night just to take my class. Afterward, they felt peaceful, had better memory and their fear of finals had disappeared.

The deep relaxation and the positive intention set at the start of the practice also brought miracles of manifestation, healing and bliss to many members of my community.

I was so happy to see such great results from my yoga teachings. And it was very fulfilling to do something positive to alleviate the stress and suffering of others.

If you learn the technique to dive within, you'll get more creativity. You'll be able to catch ideas when you expand consciousness... dive in, transcend, and all avenues of life improve.

—DAVID LYNCH

The 5th House is the house of mantras—or sacred sounds of creation that increase your intelligence and protect your mind from negativity.

A mantra is a sound equivalent to the object. This is the secret behind the mantras.

—DR. PILLAI

Jupiter and the Power of Wisdom

You cannot drive the darkness out of a room by beating at it with a stick. But if you turn on the light, the darkness will vanish as though it had never been.

—PARAMAHANSA YOGANANDA

Quick Meditation

- Choose your goal: Acquiring more wealth? Making more beautiful creations? Feeling more powerful and in control of your life? Make sure your goal is pure, ethical and it doesn't hurt anyone.
- Choose and visualize a Goddess who can bring you the fulfillment of your desire. See yourself as that Goddess. Feel her power as your own power. See her beauty as your own beauty. Feel her intelligence as your own intelligence. Feel the joy of being a powerful and beautiful Goddess.

The Goddess is in charge of giving 'Chit' or miracle consciousness. 'Chit' is the ability to know everything.

—DR. PILLAI

Meditation

- Set a timer for a desired time and close your eyes.
- Chant the OM sound of creation to increase intelligence and put light into your brain.
- Begin by chanting aloud.
- Turn inward and chant mentally.
- Relax and open your eyes.

I am deeply fulfilled by all that I do.

—LOUISE HAY

SIXTH SPIRITUAL LAW
Your Path to Well-Being and Success

When you take care of your body and follow a sensible health plan, both your body and projects will blossom. Your stamina and diligence will overcome lethargy, and your strength will defeat all competitors.

6TH HOUSE

Litigation, Enemies, Service, Hard Work, Competitors, Health

Affirmation

My health is a divine gift and I learn how to get healthier every day. My well-being brings me financial wealth. The money I spend caring for my health returns to me multiplied. I feel great and I love my work.

Planetary Ruler of the 6th House

Planets Ruling the 6th House: Mars, Saturn, and Mercury.

Mars

- Energy
- Courage
- Right Action
- Self-Discipline
- Victory
- Anger
- Aggression
- War

The planet Mars, the spiritual warrior of self-discipline and protection is one of the rulers of the sixth house. This planet's influence allows you to work harder and take powerful actions to succeed. Mars is also the planet of passion and adventure.

The dark aspects of Mars are anger and violence. So to reach your goal without making enemies, it's very important to avoid anger or engaging in destructive behavior.

We all feel anger sometimes, especially when we experience overwhelming frustration due to endless delays. Anger is a natural reaction when one faces wrongdoing from competitors. Often the enemies, however, are found within, and we interpret others' careless behavior as a personal insult. Either way, the sense of powerlessness that ensues feels quite real and painful.

Dr. Pillai teaches that anger is not a necessary ingredient for success. In fact, some brains, he says, repel anger and thoughts of scarcity and poverty. These people simply see opportunity in difficult situations. So the issue is not only biological, but also neurological.

Impatience, anger, irritation, frustration come from space and most brains receive these thoughts. So refusing and making an effort to let go of those destructive thoughts is a major step to evolution and success.

Saturn

- Hard Work
- Compassion
- Perseverance
- Humility
- Corporate CEO
- Longevity

Saturn is the planet of perseverance. Without grit and tenacity, your goals cannot easily manifest. Saturn brings you fear—which can be a motivating factor just so you don't quit before reaching your goals.

Mercury

- Intelligence
- Speech
- Writing
- Health
- Skin
- Ideas
- Details
- Cash
- Business

Mercury is a fast planet ruling speech, writing, business and detailed analysis. Mercury juggles a multitude of ideas and is changeable and restless. Mercury brings you wealth when your ideas, speech, marketing and PR campaigns are cleverly combined to gain from a profitable business.

Information and energy are inseparably connected. Have you ever noticed how, when you start paying attention to a particular word or color or object, that very thing seems to appear more often in your environment?

—DEEPAK CHOPRA

The Sixth House of Service or Volunteer Work

Real Life

In my early 30s, I was appointed to the position of co-chair for cultural events in a Chicago women's organization that included 450 members from over 60 countries.

The members' backgrounds spanned from diplomats to international educators, economists, and various other professions.

I was so thrilled to help with these events and considered it a great honor. I often met with other women in the organization—especially with my co-chair and the president, along with other chairmen from other committees.

At that time, I was also quite introverted and shy—and one of the younger members in the organization. So, I often hesitated to share my ideas and trusted the other more experienced women. Happily, our events were usually sold-out and successful.

My prior public speaking experience had been minor to that point, and the first time I spoke at an event in front of a group of about 200 members, I felt so nervous that I forgot to thank the president and my co-chair. A huge *faux pas*.

Then on a winter day that I'll never forget, I met with the president and my co-chair at an elegant women-only club.

This time we were supposed to plan future cultural and charitable events after examining the results of a recent survey conducted among our members and in the community.

After considering the sheets of paper in front of me, I felt that the method used for the survey was unclear. But to avoid a wrong assessment, I asked the president for clarifications. I felt a strange warmth on my cheeks.

Soft-spoken and chic as usual, the president slowly lifted her reading glasses off her nose, and looked straight into my eyes.

I squirmed and felt a knot in my stomach. With an unusually serious expression, she proceeded to explain the various details of our methods and goals. I began moving in my chair. Her explanation had made no sense to me.

My co-chair, a blond version of Audrey Hepburn, wearing a pastel Chanel suit—her preferred style for our meetings—came to my rescue. Or so I thought.

For a moment, she, too, gave me a serious stare, then in an irritated sounding tone, added several more instructions to follow. I didn't get any of them, but remained silent.

Even though they both regained their usual amiability and smiles, I mentally planned to leave the meeting. I began playing with my pen and move slightly in the chair and looked for the closest exit.

Soon silence reigned and we all looked down at our well-organized pile of papers waiting for attention on the Louis XVI style table.

A waitress brought a tray with macaroons. Sipping more tea, I realized that I was eating more pastries than I ordinarily would have.

I kept doodling with my pen for a seemingly long time, looked around and braced myself for a goodbye to my role as co-chair.

Then it was just me and my papers—and you could have heard a fly in the room. So I looked into the project more deeply. Since the two women's explanations had failed to clarify, I decided to rely on my own creative thinking and problem-solving. I had no other choice.

A solution came to me quickly, but it just seemed too elementary. So I bit my pen again. It was a silver pen I had received as a wedding gift. I thought, *I'd better stop biting or I'll leave a dent.*

I needed a new solution. Then I decided to put tiny dots on some key lines of the documents to remind myself of certain outcomes. I really hoped my system would work—I so wanted it to be useful, and save my reputation.

After reading my notes, I became convinced that this process would work. I tried it and retried it. I completed the task, despite my lack of any advanced math skills. I sat, sipped some more tea and waited.

About half an hour later, we were asked to read out loud our findings.

The president spoke first. Then came my turn—I read my results. The president seemed pleased and thanked me. I sat quietly.

When my co-chair spoke, the president soon interrupted her saying that something about the results seemed wrong.

My co-chair fumbled and blushed. Now that I wasn't in trouble, the whole thing didn't seem like a big deal. And we all make mistakes.

This was for me a huge learning experience, as I realized that making public mistakes wasn't the end of the world, and that it was actually okay—and there were no grave consequences in admitting a lack of understanding, as I had.

For me, this was also a victory over my fear of inadequacy. I was the only foreigner at that table and those dignified ladies were known for their talents and standing in society. My old fears about language gaps had resurfaced, I'd won, and fear had lost.

This episode is a gentle reminder for you to trust yourself and your inner resources, even in difficult situations. Yes, any work environment can become a cause of stress, but never, ever feel too embarrassed to ask questions—because questions are just stepping stones to solutions and that's how we all learn.

Studies on Success

University of Pennsylvania's studies by Angela Lee Duckworth have shown that the most important requirements for success are neither high IQ nor incredible knowledge.

In her research, in fact, she found that the greatest tools to reaching one's goals were both *passion* and *grit*—not inborn genius, not special background, not impressive doctorates, not amazing connections!

In other words, all you need is to love what you do, persevere and never take "no" for an answer, despite delays and disappointments. This process will ensure your success.

I'm convinced that about half of what separates successful entrepreneurs from the non-successful ones is pure perseverance.
—STEVE JOBS

The yogis believe that where your attention goes, your energy flows. So, you're naturally capable of energizing anything you focus on. Conversely, by pouring your energy on things you don't want, you're more likely to manifest unpleasant circumstances.

By remaining alert and paying attention to what's useful, practical, beneficial and life-enhancing, you experience wonderful changes that previously looked impossible. For example, if you wanted to own a house and yet you kept looking for rentals, or read articles on the difficulties in finding affordable real estate, you could not concentrate your energy enough to actually buy a house.

Whereas, if you focus on your desired real estate, and the many ways abundance can come into your life—you will be more likely to find opportunities to buy a lovely and affordable home for yourself.

The yogis and the Siddhas teach that to manifest what you want, you need to be totally passionate about it. Your passion and joyful emotions will give birth to what you desire.

They also advise you to keep a lovely mental image of your wanted manifestation at all times.

Real Life

Hilton's Dream:
In his book *Be My Guest,* Conrad Hilton tells the story of his childhood poverty and a seemingly impossible dream.

One day when he was just a young boy, he came across an image of the Waldorf Astoria in a newspaper—and he became so enamored with it that he cut out the image. He kept this image of the magnificent hotel on the dining table because due to his family's extreme poverty, he didn't own a desk.

The little boy looked at the image of the elegant Waldorf every day and every time he sat at the table. Finally, he made a resolution: one day he would buy the Waldorf Astoria.

As an adult, he became immensely wealthy in the hotel business. He then flew to England to make an offer to Queen Elizabeth, the owner of the Waldorf Astoria. Giving her a blank check with his signature, he asked her to write any amount of money, and he would definitely accept it.

The Queen, probably impressed with his gesture and passion, replied that she was willing to take the market value for her hotel.

This is how Hilton was able to fulfill his childhood dream. It's clear that passion and grit worked for him at all times and contributed to his becoming one of earth's richest people.

Protect Your Creations

According to the energy of the sixth house, to attract what you really love you need to stay alert, pay attention to details, write down your cherished goals (passion) and focus on them with unrelenting dedication (grit). Of course, a sure way to kill your goals is to ignore them and neglect working towards them.

The sixth house teaches that to manifest your ideal job or business, you'll need lots of energy and a prompt response to solve your problems and avoid debts. You will also need to protect your goals from forgetfulness and fatigue. Then, only decisiveness and wisdom will get you through the impasse.

- *POWER FOOD instead of Power Bar*

Because the sixth house shows that you need perfect health to meet the demands of your work and obligations, it's important that you pay close attention to your diet. Ayurveda explains that food is medicine when consumed properly.

Have you noticed how top performers in most fields eat differently? They hire experts or do their own research to learn every possible health tip. They radiate energy and enthusiasm—a subtle aura of smiley positivity surrounding their face. Many have mastered their well-being and keep a disciplined routine of work and workout.

More often than not, these individuals don't give in to cravings for unhealthy eating, drinking and other substances that weaken their resolve and concentration.

Processed food is rarely seen on their plates. They eat organic, mostly vegetarian, freshly made, simple foods. Often, they hire a cook, so they ensure that they eat only freshly made foods even when they're busy or don't feel like cooking. It takes a lot of commitment and self-discipline to stay this focused—and that's precisely what makes a difference from an *okay* to a successful performance.

It goes without saying that your good health is paramount for your mental freedom, high energy and optimum success. Of course, sometimes we don't have control over our health. Yet when we make a resolution and commit to the best possible nutrition and create a balanced routine of exercise, sleep, rest and fresh foods, our body and mind reward us with natural joy, vibrant energy and mental alertness. Moreover, in a healthier body your intuition will soar, and you'll bubble with contentment and positivity.

You will feel good in your skin and look more attractive to others. After all, most of what we call 'beautiful' is just healthy and pure—like a smooth and even complexion, sparkly eyes filled with innocence, a clear mind with positive thoughts, a fit and attractive body.

How to Deal with Enemies and Competitors

By focusing on building your skills further and ignoring others' jealousy or envy, you tap into the divine energy of the sixth house. After all, we cannot convert the entire world to our vision—neither do we need to.

Try to put among your goals excellence and authenticity. Too much strategy can make us inauthentic and can create enemies because others cannot be fooled by empty words or pretenses. A lack of sincerity will eventually surface for all to see.

To be outspoken is easy when you don't wait to speak the complete truth.

—RABINDRANATH TAGORE

So we must be as authentic as possible to be effective. Of course, skill is necessary to avoid overwork and failure. But speaking with your true voice and developing your own style will make your work more fun and details won't bog you down.

When you live merely as a strategist, your life moves like a river of sludge. When you realize your true Self, life flows effortlessly like a river of light.

—MOOJI

Increase Health and Enthusiasm

Meditation

- Sit in a quiet place and set a timer for *10 minutes*.
- Write down three bad habits that are causing you lethargy and lack of motivation.
- Next to each item in your list, write an opposite habit that will lead you to success.

Example

Problem—Overeating ice cream at nighttime. New Habit—Eating an early, light dinner and going to sleep before 10 p.m.

- Now with your eyes closed, visualize a white light. See yourself in this light as your ideal version of yourself. Put also an image that shows the lifestyle you're trying to achieve.

Example 1: You're slim, fit and your skin looks radiant. You're a fashion editor and are wearing a beautifully fitting white dress with matching high-heeled pumps. Your hair is shiny and styled by your favorite celebrity hairstylist. A lovely gold bracelet shines on your wrist sending waves of golden rays across the room.

Example 2: You own the organic vegetable farm of your dreams. See yourself in cute rubber boots, stretch denims, looking happy, healthy and even radiant. See the fruit trees and the people who help you run this farm.

Example 3: You're sitting in your designer office surrounded by your efficient, happy and capable team. Everyone is upbeat and shares positive comments and useful feedback. You joyfully celebrate your first million revenue from your consulting business by inviting the whole team to dinner in a lovely restaurant.

Reminder

Try to imagine an outrageous dream and goal. There's no need to be overly realistic. Make your dream big!

- Relax. Slowly, slowly open your eyes.

Carefully Choose Your Audience

The sixth house will test your willpower and sometimes you might not get support even from loved ones or friends.

What will you do then? You must believe in yourself, even if no one else does. Trust that if you have a deep, passionate yearning for something, you'll meet with success. You must also be willing to fight others' doubts.

Have you ever experienced this?

While eating your breakfast or taking a morning walk, you get a sudden epiphany. Or maybe you had a dream from which came a flash of intuition.

When you acted on your epiphany and intuition, you found inexplicable coincidences that confirmed you were on the right path to fulfilling your dream. You now foresee a great future for yourself through this new idea—and you know exactly how to implement it. You enjoy visualizing your dream in all its details—scents, colors, people in it, lovely feelings, pleasant emotions, and even its location.

You want to jump up and down with delight because you know this creation already exists—you can feel it.

Then excitedly, you decide to share your new idea and project with a loyal friend or family members.

Their facial expressions frowning with doubt pierce your heart. Then comes their blank stare poorly disguised by a weak, *Nice*. How do you feel? Is it like a bucket of icy water being splashed on your happiness?

I learned this lesson over and over again—because I liked and trusted my friends, I often shared the excitement for a new project, but my peers' skepticism would leave a mark on my confidence. While some of us can feel more self-assured and are able to recover quickly from lack of support—the truth is that we usually maintain a subconscious record of others' skepticism.

So beware of kissing and telling too soon, because a negative response, whether it's apparent or hidden, can harm your dream. Then your own logic and skepticism—which are often regular features of our conscious, subconscious or unconscious thinking—begin to match your confidant's doubts.

At that point, we risk losing both momentum and courage. And even if you persist in your attempt and work towards your dream, you'll need twice as much enthusiasm and self-trust to succeed.

Sadly, more often than not we just give up on our tender, precious dreams.

So you could try to share your wishes and projects that you've already manifested, unless one of the two following conditions is present:

- This person's help is paramount for the realization of your goal through financial support, expertise or connections.
- That person shares the same dream with you, which usually happens when couples, business partners, or specific group members share the same goals, aesthetic, desires and ideas.

Show up to Receive a Miracle

Mars shows that it's the *weightlifting* in the sixth house that makes our muscles stronger—not sitting on the couch, no matter how well stuffed or well-designed it might be. We need courage, determination and action.

Real Life

Suit up and show up—this simple yet powerful saying has always supported me in my career when I felt overwhelmed by overwork or pessimism. I've followed it and it worked.

Get help from a coach, trainer or specialist if you need to. In the case of fitness, don't despair if you cannot afford a trainer—that's what video downloads are for. Just suit up and show up in front of your TV or PC screen. Try to have fun and look for a variety of choices—that's the way of *Mercury*.

We also need to save our precious energy and avoid exposure to activities and thoughts that deplete energy. For example, it was lucky that I never liked gossip. I would feel uncomfortable growing up while hearing my peers talk negatively about absent others.

It was boring for me and I especially felt sorry for the victims of gossip who weren't there to defend themselves. I even lost some friends for my lack of interest in gossiping—I know, because they actually told me.

Instead of gossiping or watching TV shows with some peers—I spent time alone. I then realized that I had more energy and time to do the things I really loved—going to dance class, working out, studying and reading.

And my trusted, successful friends didn't gossip either. Filling the mind with useless and negative thoughts about others, it turns out, is an occupation for frustrated people who don't value their own time and don't like themselves.

Of course, after a painful experience, we need to call a good friend for insights and emotional support.

In my experience, to heal from a bad experience caused by a thoughtless person, silence and time alone work wonders. Of course, make sure to ask for help if you cannot get over your hurt on your own. So the sixth house is also about what is both unpleasant and difficult, yet will eventually contribute to your success and victory.

The sixth house energy shows the positive developments from staying disciplined and courageously stand up for yourself.

Planetary Recipe for Success

Standing up for ourselves (through help from defensive Mars) with humility and a service-oriented attitude (Saturn's domain), and allowing flexibility in your plans (as Mercury teaches), you will be in a better position to win.

The creation of a thousand forests is one acorn.
—RALPH WALDO EMERSON

Real Life

I worked in public relations with an extremely talented colleague, Helen (not her real name). From day one, Helen exuded assertiveness, self-confidence but also some noticeable aggressiveness. While I was in awe of her intelligence and skills, I often avoided her because of her commanding tone.

I would ask myself, *Why is she trying to control me and everything I do?* I began disliking seeing her or talking to her. But, for some reason, I kept hoping this relationship would improve. I wanted to be on her good side, so I sincerely complimented on her good traits and efficient work.

My non-discriminating attitude must have worked because soon she accepted my offer to help her with some projects. She even began asking me to join her in meetings with her new clients.

One evening, as we worked late to complete a project, Helen finally spoke more openly about her beliefs and fears, and the reason why she often put up a tough façade.

People are sharks, she said with conviction. I listened in silence. She continued to explain her point in a hurt tone, *to be successful you need to defend yourself from sharks out there. And for this, you must become a shark yourself.*

I could now see how this belief had been bringing havoc in her life and even at the office, and was likely the reason she often tried to dominate others. I felt compassion for her, but I also had a need for authenticity. So I said that I was sorry she'd been hurt, but I believed that most human beings were inherently good.

Also, I thought that stress and fear made people act out in the workplace, and believed that sincere respect, kindness, caring, and expecting the best from each person were better ways to respond to difficult situations. I also believed in avoiding competition and creating a safe place for mutual trust and cooperation.

We remained silent for some time. I felt that her self-protective shield was hiding her more genuine emotions. Because of her hurt, she'd lost some of her original enthusiasm and vision that could have made her work more creative and satisfying.

I knew that she suffered from a stomach ulcer, despite her being only 30 years old. From my studies of *Ayurveda*, I learned that ulcers were usually associated with stress and suppressed emotions, leading to anger and excessive body heat. She couldn't control her temper even with our soft-spoken owner of the public relations agency.

So I suggested meditation and yoga, which had helped me get healthier and manage negative emotions. These practices had also helped me acquire better self-esteem, which had been low after leaving my country and moving to the U.S.

I knew that Helen juggled her work duties, caring for her new baby, and her role as a wife—a common situation among working women. Fortunately, our conversation calmed her down and I started to enjoy working with her.

I knew that behind her irritating traits, Helen was kind, and she had eagerly helped me in some key projects, teaching me invaluable strategies for my work as a publicist.

So I told her that if she could just trust her exceptional capacities, she'd be happier and gentler with herself and others. She listened quietly to what I said. I had feared that she might get upset, yet she didn't.

A great vision emerges from silent contemplation.

—ANONYMOUS

In summary, the sixth house requires attention, dedication, selflessness, and patience. And I believe that meditation is the most important tool to face the challenges of the sixth house and overcome them!

In fact, I've observed the miracles from meditation in countless individuals, including my students. In my case over the past 25 years, I've kept a regular meditation practice, which among numerous benefits, taught me how to work smarter. My best ideas, in fact, came during meditation without even looking for an idea—and this was an exciting discovery.

Also, I found that meditation can put us in touch with our true feelings, reduces stress, which is the cause of over 70 percent of doctors' visits in the U.S. alone. From stress, spring allergies, anger, fear, and a weaker immune system.

Moreover, meditation can help us become more authentic, open, transparent, creative, compassionate, and last but not least, intelligent.

SEVENTH SPIRITUAL LAW
Your Love and Relationships

As you give your love to others and make them happy, your happiness grows exponentially. Your fairness and gentleness towards your partner and others in your life lead to harmonious relationships, enhanced creativity, great connections, and a satisfying social life.

7TH HOUSE

Spouse, Desire, Enjoyment, Sex, Committed Relationships, Business Partners, Social Life

Love each other unconditionally and you'll be enlightened.

—DR. PILLAI

Affirmation

My relationships express my divine origins. As I evolve, my relationships become more loving and enjoyable every day.

The seventh house is focused on relationships, harmony, finding compatible partners and cooperative co-workers, and enjoying happy social connections. Diplomacy and fairness are also qualities belonging to the seventh house, along with commitment to cement a union between two people in love, or business partners.

Planetary Ruler of the 7th House

The planet of the 7th house is loving Venus.

VENUS

- Beauty
- Happiness
- Luxury
- Arts
- Creativity
- Love
- Romance
- Diplomacy
- Relationships
- Entertainment

Venus is the planet of relationships, beauty, lovely design, luxury, fancy cars, love and romance. Venus can bring earthly joys and sensual pleasures. Relationships are meant to be equal and fair. As you choose to make your partner happy, he or she will make you happy.

Have you ever felt disconnected from love? Were you unable to feel love and could only feel sadness and disappointment? Or worse, did you feel numb and didn't know what to do? Perhaps this happened after the loss of a relationship. In yogic terms, that means that your heart center was temporarily blocked. This is the point in the middle of your chest, and an important vortex of energy, love and intelligence.

Yet Venus can bring back happiness and new relationships into your life, healing your sorrows and helping you forget the past. Venus brings harmony in interactions with others, artistic and physical beauty, a lovely home or car, jewelry, and enjoyable entertainment. But love, more than anything else, can heal a broken heart.

Venus seeks pleasure and connection through a satisfying social life and happy partnerships. With the help of Venus, you can select your life partner based on mutual attraction, commitment, shared interests and compatibility.

This exchange of love and pleasure can become more sublime when our expectations from the other person are fair, we focus on respect, and bring happiness to our partner.

Needless to say, harmony with your business associates is also important. By finding win-win solutions and agreements, you can experience more happiness both at home and at work.

In fact, the Rishis said that true joy comes from loving and respecting everyone. Love is the highest vibration.

Allow yourself to receive love unconditionally from others. Give love from your heart unconditionally to yourself and others and you will experience the highest state of consciousness possible.

—SRI SRI RAVI SHANKAR

Happiness for No Reason

"Be happy now" say the yogis. Unconditional happiness without a special reason is an ideal state of harmony with all beings and all creation. This is the highest expression of Venus.

The Unconditional Love of the Moon vs. The Conditional Love of Venus

It's important to note that the ancient Vedic sages taught that Venus rules equal love and not unconditional love—as you have seen in the fourth house and the Moon, which signifies motherly love and safety.

Today, too many enter marriage with the expectation of unconditional, motherly love. That's one of the reasons for so many broken hearts and ended relationships.

In ancient times, love and attraction were only some of the components for a lasting marriage relationship—as commitment, common goals, agreements, harmony, diplomacy, shared pleasures, and polite manners were other necessary, cementing elements.

So Venus does not bring motherly or fatherly feelings of love for romantic and marriage partners. Venus' natural reserve must be bridged with activities that both partners enjoy. Small sacrifices that benefit your partner's needs can bring a lasting and happy relationship. But both partners must make equal amounts of efforts and commitment.

Keep in mind that by extending our love to all beings and all creation, our capacity to give and receive love in a relationship will grow, too.

In Vedic astrology, we call this expansion "the exaltation of Venus," which happens when Venus is auspiciously placed in Pisces—a sign ruled by Jupiter.

Romantic Love is Just the Beginning

When you feel the attraction and desire to be with another person, you're experiencing the initial spark of love through infatuation. After this initial stage in the relationship, love must grow through devotion, commitment, and harmony.

Meditation

Ask yourself what qualities you'd like to see in your romantic partner or business associates. Because Venus is the ruler of these interactions that require a give-and-take attitude, you must be willing to offer the same to them.

- Make a short list of the non-negotiable characteristics you need. For example, for you to consider a relationship with this person, you'll need to see politeness, cleanliness, generosity, attractive clothes, a happy and positive demeanor, harmony and gentleness. Or list other qualities you'd like.
- Now close your eyes. Mentally scan your body. Put your attention on the heart center (or heart chakra).
- Mentally tell your heart to relax. Think of someone you'd like to forgive. If you remember an unpleasant episode with a person at work or in your personal relationship—just acknowledge it. Then let it go.
- Visualize white light coming and cleansing that situation further. Say, *Now we are both free.*
- When you do this meditation regularly, that negative memory will lose its power over you and will disappear. You'll even find that in just a few weeks, positive memories will replace the bad ones. And your capacity to experience happiness will grow.

The heart has its own intelligence. The heart has, in fact, the highest intelligence. The mind within the heart is full of compassion.

—DR. PILLAI

As a house of desire and relationship, the seventh house teaches you that cultivating meaningful relationships with others is paramount for your happiness and the fulfillment of your desires. Similarly, your happiness at work increases by getting along with everyone or finding compatible associates.

Openness Brings Happiness

After being hurt, it's fairly common to temporarily shut down and feel you can never love again. But by staying alert to the infinite opportunities for happiness with others, it becomes much easier to find new love.

It's also important to commit to your happiness by choosing harmony over battle, compromise over conquering, diplomacy over cutting words—so it takes alertness and openness to reach the final goal and form happy and long-lasting relationships.

Meaningful Synchronicity

Another useful, spiritual step is staying open to receiving clues from your surroundings and others. Meaningful coincidences are positive indications that you've been heard—and that the universe is helping you find a compatible and loving partner.

Apparently, when you make a decision or *sankalpa*—as the yogis call a strong intention—and remain positive and open, spontaneous events will orchestrate the fulfillment of your wish. In the Vedic tradition, this phenomenon is called *"ritam-bhara pragya,"* and stems from the interconnectedness of all creation.

Example of Synchronicity

Just as you're making plans for your upcoming vacation, you suddenly think that you'd really love to go golfing.

Yet you don't own a membership to a country club and wonder how you can possibly fulfill that desire.

Then, you randomly open a magazine and your eyes fall on an image of a golf course with two people golfing. As you observe this image, your desire to play golf with a friend grows stronger.

Later that day, you take a walk in the park and unexpectedly, you come across a former business partner that you haven't seen in years. After a brief conversation, he invites you to his country club for a golf game and lunch next week. You're delighted at this unexpected fulfillment of your wish.

Authentic Desires

Knowing your desires is important for your happiness, because it can help you identify priorities and whether they can really bring you joy in the long run.

Authentic passion is the excitement you feel when you've discovered what you love. You're connected with something larger than yourself, something magical, something sacred.

—KHAIRU DHANANI

Meditation

- Sit in a quiet place. Close your eyes. Ask yourself: *What do I want?* The truth of what you really want comes first. It can be something that may appear too grandiose, yet you don't need to scale down your dream.
- Visualize your dream environment with your ideal relationship or social network. Every day, write any coincidence that can lead to the fulfillment of your desire.
- Keep a *coincidence journal* handy. No coincidence is too small.
- Keep your faith alive and trust that your wish will definitely manifest.
- Choose to be kinder and more loving with all the people you meet. Even on challenging days, recommit to this intention.

When you meet some people and you come back feeling positive about yourself and your life, thank these people for being there for you.

—AMMA

What You Think Manifests

The yogis warn us that every thought we think is likely to manifest. Words, too, manifest their energetic meaning—because they originate from thoughts. So if we want happiness, it's absolutely necessary to select only positive words and good intentions at all times.

Whatever you think becomes a reality in the invisible space-time complex of your soul. Then this manifests in life after an appropriate lapse of time. That's why it's very, very important to be positive.

—DR. PILLAI

Real Life

We often choose partners based on idealistic imagery and hopes. For many young women, a version of a fairytale-like Prince Charming—handsome, kind, rich and protective—is the aspired model.

At 20, I got engaged to someone who looked just like this Prince. A year later, however, this relationship ended just on the verge of marriage. Sadness and hurt feelings on both sides and dismayed parents were the results. Yet, I was just 21 and apparently, I wasn't ready to get married so young.

A year after the painful ending of my engagement, I began spending more time with my friends and meeting new people.

One summer night in Rome, I had dinner at the house of a female friend who had invited a small group of our childhood friends. I kept quiet and avoided entering into conversation with anyone. I just stared at the lovely Roman sunset, looking glorious from my friend's penthouse.

At the dining table, as I sat next to a boy about my age, I didn't pay much attention to others, finding myself in the grips of nostalgia and memories of happy times with my ex-fiancé.

Suddenly, Giacomo, whom I'd just met, asked me: "Where would you like to go to the beach tomorrow?" Absent-mindedly I answered: "Côte d'Azur." He seemed nice, but I had no desire of going to the beach with him or anyone else. I blurted out a place far enough to make a date more unlikely. I also felt a bit guilty for answering that way, as I had no desire to go to France either. I'm sure I was giving out a silent message that said: "I'm not interested."

Yet Giacomo politely said, "Fine. Should I pick you up at noon?" I really thought he wasn't talking seriously, but I agreed on the time. Later I asked my friends about Giacomo—they all told me that he was a great guy, honest, well-educated, single and really kind.

Every girl has a different name for a similar character who's kind, handsome, loyal, protective, and more. I began to feel hope that I'd just met such a person. Giacomo had impressed me with his good manners, good looks and lack of affectation.

The next morning, he called me and reminded me to pack a suitcase because we would be spending the weekend with his family in Beaulieu. Was that okay? "Yes," I said.

He was on time. He picked me up and we drove to a private airport near Rome. There, his mother and little sister were waiting for us on their family jet. Two uniformed pilots, a captain and a first officer, were ready for take-off. The luxurious environment and Giacomo's warm attention towards me were Prince-Charming style, no doubt, and a perfect expression of Venus and the seventh house. Giacomo's mother was delightful—she smiled and looked genuinely friendly. So I felt almost at home.

We were served appetizers and soft drinks. Talking to Giacomo was so relaxing—he had none of the high-strung energy of my ex-fiancé, whose restlessness made me fear that our relationship wouldn't last.

Giacomo instead was calm, serious and a joy to talk with. He did not engage in sarcastic remarks. I'd always felt uncomfortable around sarcastic or ironic talks. He was poised, kind of like me, but this was definitely a funny way to get to know him—in the presence of his mother and sister.

Soon we arrived at the Nice airport. A driver wearing a blue beret was waiting for us in a big, dark-blue Jaguar.

Then, we drove for some time and finally reached a yacht, where another crew dressed in white had been waiting for us with our lunch ready to be served. We sat and ate in the shade. Giacomo and I refused the champagne served by the waiter.

This was really exciting: we both didn't like drinking alcohol! He certainly looked more and more like my ideal man. Yet after some time, the lack of familiarity and the fact that I barely knew him made me feel uncomfortable and out of place.

But Giacomo was not like other rich boys I knew. He noticed my uneasiness and asked me warmly, "Are you okay?" A few, but thoughtful words. He was simple and I loved that.

He seemed sensitive to my feelings and constantly checked with me to make sure I was comfortable. He then asked me if I wanted to drive to town. "Yes, I'd really like to." We drove around the lovely coast.

We had a great time. The details of that day are still vivid in my memory. Was I falling in love again? The beautiful landscape, the colors and scents of flowers, plants, the sun, sea and sky were soothing to my aching heart.

I remember this as the day that we actually met—because our conversation the night before had been so casual and brief. We shopped, laughed, shared memories, and I had a great feeling that I wanted to be with him forever. I chose a pair of espadrilles and flat sandals.

In the following days, we were always together, except for the time Giacomo engaged in water sports, which I disliked and found scary. But I loved swimming with him. When we dived off the boat I felt happy and protected in the chilled, deep-blue seawater.

In the next few days, I secretly put him through a final test. A yacht nearby was hosting a small group of young people. Two girls, thin and tall much like fashion models, appeared so lovely in their bikinis, lightly bronzed bodies and long hair glowing when they tilted their heads and laughed in blinding sunlight.

My ex-fiancé had a habit that caused me much discomfort and embarrassment—he liked to stare at pretty girls even in my presence. I secretly detested this behavior, but I was too shy to confront him openly.

Giacomo, instead, seemed oblivious to the girls. "Don't you think they're beautiful?" I asked. He shrugged: "They're too loud and too thin for my taste," he said, "You're more beautiful."

This reply made me instantly feel like the prettiest girl on earth, and I began thinking that he was my ideal man. He would tell me: "Look at you. No makeup. How can you be so beautiful?"

We decided to go out at night, but I hadn't brought any elegant clothes from home, as I had packed very lightly. And as we were getting ready to attend a dinner party nearby, I regretted having nothing special to wear.

Giacomo's mother came to the rescue—she asked me to choose among her lovely evening gowns. I picked a silk, navy blue one that reached my ankles and fit me perfectly. She then insisted that I wear some of her precious jewelry. I chose a delicate gold necklace studded with diamonds and lapis lazuli with matching earrings. I felt like a princess.

During my entire stay, Giacomo and I had an amazing time—everything seemed magical. Back in Rome, my friends were happy to know about my new relationship and asked many questions.

I kept thinking—*Giacomo didn't flirt with other attractive girls*. For me, this was his best quality. Finally, I was healing from my past failed relationship.

Then one day, my ex-fiancé called me. He told me that he missed me terribly and that he wanted a second chance. He asked me to meet him. I felt myself literally shaking on the phone and my heart pounding.

I accepted on a whim—more due to the strong emotions of the moment than for a deep feeling of love. At that age, I knew nothing about the notion of *karmic attachment* and its dangers.

Reluctantly, I broke up with Giacomo and told him that I wanted to try to mend my relationship with my ex-fiancé. He seemed sad, but also understanding. Yet after a few months, it became apparent that I would never be happy with my ex. So my new engagement ended, and this time permanently.

As for Giacomo, I never had the courage to contact him again. Another year passed, and I met him on a plane going to Milan. He looked so grownup and handsome in a gray suit.

He barely said a cool hello to me and disappeared from my life. It took me some time to get over the feeling that I'd missed an opportunity to be with Prince Charming.

It took me an even longer time to learn that those thoughts of loss and longing were the result of karmic imprints—which eventually manifest in the form of events.

According to Vedic astrology, our likes and dislikes from past lives create our future. This principle also takes into consideration our free will. Yet we are normally unaware of the reasons why we choose one partner over another. Then, when things go wrong we often feel powerless or blame others for our bad luck.

And while my image of the ideal partner has changed dramatically over the years—basic qualities such as intelligence, kindness, loyalty, integrity, spiritual evolution, compassion, and faithfulness remain important.

If you still haven't met your soulmate, follow the information of the seventh house to understand the qualities that you're *really* looking for. This information will also improve your current relationship.

[Throughout the universe] The connecting principle, the force that expands our consciousness beyond ourselves, appears to be love.

—DR. JOHN E. MACK

The Rishis taught us that good relationships are based primarily on similarities, compatibility and common aims. Ideally, the two partners should evolve simultaneously and have similar (if not the same) spiritual practices.

We often face great confusion in matters of the seventh house: a breakup, the loss of a loved one, a new relationship, a life-changing event—can cloud our clarity and we can get temporarily off track.

Although relationships don't come with a guarantee—Vedic astrology can offer amazing help to identify a compatible life partner and the closest thing to your Prince Charming or Ideal Woman.

The information revealed by a compatibility report based on the two birth charts of the partners is accurate and allows the matching of your unique traits with compatible versions of another soul. There are easy yet crucial points that can predict whether a person will make you happy.

This celestial technology could save couples from heartbreak, and contribute to long-lasting relationship happiness.

Meditation

This meditation will reveal subconscious imprints that can help you choose a compatible partner.

- Sit in a quiet place and close your eyes. Take a few moments to remember the qualities you're proudest of. (Perhaps you're naturally kind to others. Or you're a gifted writer or great at math. Or your natural warmth easily attracts people.)
- Then acknowledge the qualities that could be holding you back or causing problems with others.

Note: Acknowledging doesn't mean self-bashing. Simply list the characteristics that you'd rather let go of and that aren't serving you well. Be compassionate and gentle with yourself.

- Mentally place your negative qualities (example: selfishness, indecisiveness, anger, etc.) in an imaginary paper bag. Visualize yourself burning the bag and say: "I let go of what I don't need anymore, and let God take care of it."
- Now with your eyes still closed, visualize your ideal partner. Mentally list all the qualities you want in him or her. Be sincere. Imagine him or her (examples: creative, loyal, kind, generous, good looking, humorous, compassionate).
- You can also write these qualities down in a journal.
- Relax and open your eyes.

Every day try to incorporate one of those positive qualities in your behavior. Which of these qualities do you already own? Try to cultivate those awesome qualities that are still weak in you, and begin to become the person that you'd love to be with.

You can also look for a qualified and certified Vedic astrologer or coach to discover whether a prospective partner is really compatible. And find out which planets in your birth chart support or hinder a loving relationship. The astrologer can then advise you accordingly and suggest appropriate remedies.

Love is the only reality and it is not a mere sentiment. It is the ultimate truth that lies at the heart of creation.

—RABINDRANATH TAGORE

EIGHTH SPIRITUAL LAW
Your Transformation and Longevity

After a difficult experience, you can rise again like a phoenix, finding new ways of manifesting your dreams. All you need to do is search deeper into yourself. What you'll discover is that you're an embodied perfection of God.

Metaphysics, Disease, Transformation, Fears, In-Laws, Research, Psychology, Other People's Wealth

---

Karma is just thoughts that then translate themselves into action and experience.

—DR. PILLAI

Affirmation

I now uncover my hidden powers. I choose a pain-free and joyous life. In the past, I created my struggles, and now I choose different thoughts and new actions that lead me to a huge treasure. Every day, I'm creating my ideal life.

Planetary Ruler of the 8th House

The Planet of the eighth house is Saturn, the ruler of longevity, hard work, CEOs, compassion, wisdom, maturity, perseverance.

The eighth house represents loss and transformation. It also shows the financial and spiritual gains that can become available to you after a loss—such as wealth from an inheritance, a bank, a loan, but also from your spouse or in-laws.

The eighth house can signify great sorrow. Yet your suffering can become the motivating force that leads you to a positive transformation.

A heavy heart and deep resentfulness are common reactions after a major loss. Even Ayurveda, the branch of yoga governing healing, says that grief aggravates Pitta: the fire element within the heart chakra, which is the seat of our emotions.

So we often get angry even at ourselves, lose self-respect, and self-esteem after failing to reach our goals.

Real Life

When I got married and left Rome I didn't foresee that I would feel the absence of my family and friends.

131

Initially, my life became very difficult in Chicago. My husband worked hard at his family business, spending up to six days a week at the headquarters of the company. I knew no one and was also pregnant with our first child.

My days seemed lonely and somewhat depressing. My in-laws had left soon after our wedding to head to their condo in warmer Florida. They would come back in May. However, at their return, they would mostly play golf or bridge, or spend time with their many friends.

The birth of our first child didn't ease my situation. I was nursing my baby, and in the first few weeks, I spent my days at home with the nurse we had hired to help me. As it turned out, this woman would talk on the phone for most of the day, and stole some pieces of my jewelry.

Worse, I felt isolated in a city whose cold climate wears down even natives. Gone were the days of Rome's warm and mild winters.

Fortunately, the birth of my first baby brought me much joy. Yet my mother couldn't come visit me—my stepdad had been unwell.

Then when my son turned a year old, I finally began to enjoy my new life.

I made some new friends through my husband's acquaintances. My mother-in-law eventually suggested that I volunteer at the local museum of contemporary art. For a few months, I underwent the art studies and training that qualified me as a *docent*. My past knowledge of art history proved very useful in this new environment.

This volunteer position became instrumental to my awakening to a new reality in the city's artistic and social life. And through the museum, I could also do rewarding work that benefitted my community.

Overall, that period remains in my mind as a difficult time. But the positive transformation that followed taught me that I can face even extreme change and eventually become stronger and renewed.

Life is as You Choose it to Be

Although the yogis know this, most people are shocked to hear that if you have no money, you yourself have chosen this experience. In fact, thoughts due to prior conditioning or karma create inner barriers to happiness or wealth of which we are seldom aware.

The yogis also offer many techniques to help us overcome these *karmic*, or subconscious imprints.

Dr. Pillai explains that karma is a mindset—or repetitive thoughts so deeply rooted in our subconscious mind that we barely notice them.

Some other thoughts are inherited genetically from our ancestors—and there is scientific research proving this.

Letting Go

Have you ever tried to forget a painful event, only to see its memory resurface again and again? The eighth house highlights our perceived helplessness in stopping emotional pain or material loss. This perception is actually a sign that we must work to regain our power. In fact, the fear stemming from that painful event could hold you hostage, until you realize that you don't need to suffer anymore.

At any moment—after experiencing some inevitable grief—you can reinterpret that event in a more positive way that leads you to healing and profound gains.

Do you remember, for example, a time when a painful loss turned out to be a blessing in disguise? Did that event become a springboard to a better opportunity? It happens more often than we dare admit.

We also forget that our failures make us stronger and more resilient. Even when we touch bottom, a solution eventually appears.

For example, after a long period of denial, you might realize that you've been in a toxic relationship, feeling depressed, inadequate, and helpless. Leaving that relationship may initially cause much sorrow and a terrible sense of failure.

But then you begin to enjoy your new freedom and control over your destiny. You might meet a better, more compatible partner, and wonder why you remained so long in that old, unhappy relationship.

Transformation means that you tap into areas of your hidden skills and divine qualities, letting go of that which didn't serve your highest good. This should be a celebration—yet in our obfuscated view we usually perceive it as a terrible event.

This was proved in a recent survey, as in a list of the top ten most stressful events in life, retirement and marriage scored seventh and tenth respectively.

Yet too many people retire from occupations they hated, which required long commutes and barely paid their bills.

Similarly, many singles suffer from solitude. Also, in the West, people are usually free to choose their life partner—the man or woman they love.

So why is marriage listed seventh as a prime stress-inducing change, coming right after tragic events such as the death of a close family member or spouse?

A fitting answer is that our attachment to the status quo is so strong that it keeps us from creating the life of our dreams.

We all have this peculiar habit of resisting change—even very positive change. That is why many people remain attached to a lifestyle, job, or relationship that brings them mostly unhappiness.

The events of the eighth house can help us break an unnecessary attachment, and become more mature and conscious.

Why Do Bad Things Happen to Good People?

We've all experienced at least one event in which someone has stolen our property, inheritance, peace of mind or joy.

However, anything that we're experiencing today, both good and bad, happens for two main reasons:

- Karma or the law of cause and effect.
- A need to learn self-trust, and realize your divinity and infinite potential.

If someone has stolen your money, for example, it's a devastating event. Perhaps you've trusted an acquaintance or family member, and the theft points to your need to be more cautious. This will teach you to protect yourself in your future dealings.

The spiritual reason for unpleasant experiences is also a need to learn compassion for those who are suffering under similar circumstances.

Unfortunately, we often become careless when life is good to us, and we risk losing our humanness and sympathy for the underprivileged. We sometimes forget others' suffering when we focus on our happiness.

But Saturn shakes our confidence, and teaches us compassion and perseverance.

I've suffered enormous money losses in my life—primarily because I've trusted too much—especially my siblings. This has taught me that simply sharing your genetic pool with someone doesn't necessarily bring you loving and safe connections.

In fact, we're perfectly capable of forming truly beautiful relationships, and deep friendship with others who aren't related by blood or culture.

Spiritual Solution

I truly believe that only a spiritual solution can bring healing at the deepest level.

- Don't rush the healing process.
- Don't suppress anger, sorrow or other negative emotions.
- Don't unleash your anger in destructive ways. While it's a natural part of healing, expressing excessive anger can actually cause you and others more suffering.
- Always reach out, if you need to talk and find appropriate help.
- Turn to God and trust that God knows your suffering and is already helping you move forward by bringing you something better.
- Help others—the sooner you shift your focus from your suffering to those who are the most unfortunate in society, the faster healing will occur.
- Trust that you'll soon find the treasure and rewards hidden behind your pain and the path to something or someone wonderful.
- Celebrate even small victories every day.
- Create new neurons with positive thoughts and rewire your brain for happiness.
- Forgive yourself and others to relinquish attachment to your pain or people who have hurt you.

Your forgiveness, along with proper distance and boundaries, will protect you. You'll then be able to leave the cycle of suffering and you'll get spiritual merit or good karma—from which springs all good fortune, according to the yogis and Vedic astrology.

Belief in karma is an evolutionary stage in spiritual life and it leads to enlightenment.

—K. N. RAO

You are the master of your life. You're God. You have the power to create any new experiences of your choice. Pain and hatred steal your power—so forgiveness and compassion are better tools for building your future happiness.

Remember—you don't have to forgive someone's terrible actions in order to forgive that person. You're simply saying:

"We are done! I let you go and we're both free."

Eventually, you will win over your pain and you'll find new strength and powerful solutions.

Yet if complete forgiveness is slow to come, you can begin with the following affirmation to create a mental environment for forgiveness:

This experience came from my karmic attachment to you. I forgive you and let you go. Now this is your karma—and you'll have to answer your Creator for it. Yet I seek no revenge and I free myself.

Repeat it out loud as many times as you need—every day, if necessary. Then, trust in divine justice and let it go. Use your retrieved freedom to create a life that you truly love. Good things will happen to you.

Spiritual Perspective

Some people will love you. Some will have problems with you. Some will be your enemies.

—DR. PILLAI

There's an immensely valuable treasure in the eight house. It's very difficult to escape some predestined inclinations, likes and dislikes, but it's possible to transform yourself by becoming more alert and change your karma—which is made of old thoughts. In fact, not only do we think 35 to 50 thoughts a minute, but we recycle most of them.

Instead, we could choose from an incredible amount of possible actions that can help us make the best of what happens to us.

Feeling victimized—although a normal and understandable reaction during shocking and life-changing events—will take away all your power to see the situation as an opportunity to better your life.

A spiritual solution works a bit like the saying, "If life gives you lemons, make lemonade." And maybe you could market the lemonade, sell it, and become a wealthy entrepreneur!

So rewrite mentally (or even in a journal) your painful experience, and create a more positive outlook and happy outcome.

Be Like the Caterpillar

Be courageous. Between the caterpillar and the butterfly, the true heroic feat of transformation is done by the caterpillar, because it takes lots of effort to become a splendid butterfly.

- Choose to let attachment to the past go. Write it down, say it out loud—any form of refusal to continue holding on to pain will work.
- Remain alert to avoid a repetition of the old habit.

How to Transform Your Life from Pain to Joy

Many scientists believe we only use 2 percent of our DNA. We can program the remaining DNA through certain key sounds: 'AH' and 'OO'. They're the sounds of incredible intelligence and energy.

—DR. PILLAI

Meditation

- Set a timer for 15 minutes.
- Sit in a quiet place.
- Close your eyes.
- Put your attention on your forehead.
- Mentally say the sound *AH*.
- Then mentally repeat *OO*.
- Again, chant the sounds *AH, AH, AH*.
- Now: *OO, OO, OO*.
- Continue alternating these in sets of three. *AH, AH, AH. OO, OO, OO* until the timer rings.
- Then relax and slowly open your eyes.
- You can repeat this technique every time you feel a negative emotion come up.

This meditation will bring you new opportunities by changing your thoughts. This technique can be an invaluable springboard to your happiness.

You'll then become like flowers or grass after the rain: lovelier and your colors more vibrant. As the rain soaks the ground, new, greener vegetation will grow.

You'll shine with more experience and new wisdom to improve your life. You'll be more polished and fabulous, just as you were born to be.

A new state of consciousness is emerging. We have suffered enough!
—ECKHART TOLLE

Do What it Takes to Restore Your Happiness

Don't worry about the situation of the world. You must be very happy, very, very happy! Only through happiness and waves of bliss, you will be able to help your country and the entire world in an automatic manner. You will remain ever invincible when you don't allow anything to obscure your happiness.
—MAHARISHI MAHESH YOGI

Real Life

I'd just finished teaching my *restorative yoga* class—and my students were slowly coming out of *Shavasana*, the final relaxation technique on the floor. I began rolling up my mat and was elated when a woman said out loud that it was the best yoga class she'd ever taken.

A few minutes later, I opened the attendance book to enter the number of students in the health club's log. I penned down—three.

On that night, I sadly recognized my failure in motivating students for what I called "true" yoga. My yoga routine, in fact, was based on ancient techniques from *Kriya Yoga* and *Patanjali's Raja Yoga*, which included 15 to 20 minutes of final meditation.

The pace of the class was slow and meditative. Being a passionate athlete who exercised 3 hours daily—I fell in love with yoga and its perfection, being able to heal myself on several levels from stress and work-related issues.

I wanted to help others with my discoveries and give the good news that there was more to yoga than mere "Vinyasa." Vinyasa is a yoga style based on a routine of vigorous poses that ancient Indian sages had designed for celibate male monks—it was a one-size-fits-all sequence that was often injurious to practitioners.

Over the years, I'd noticed that modern yoga in the U.S. was causing more harm than good. Even my private students—all medical doctors—were concerned by the growing number of yoga-related injuries they saw.

So I made it a point to teach only classes that were both gentle and transformative through meditation and awareness.

Unfortunately, gym goers weren't too excited by my new (actually, *very ancient*) style and during my class tried to squeeze their favorite Vinyasa poses into the other *asanas*. When I ignored these attempts at changing my sequence and teachings, some began deserting my class.

I knew that the health club owner was strict about the minimum number of people needed to keep the class in the schedule: at least five attendees.

That night for the first time, I'd failed to meet the attendance requirement. Of course, it didn't help that it was on a snowy night and the last class of the day was mine. In fact, I'd been hired to teach the late-night class at 8 p.m. That night I finally threw in the proverbial towel—and quit my job.

Driving home in the dark streets, sliding slightly on fresh snow, I felt sad like after a terrible loss. On the way, I was stopped by a police officer flashing his car's blue and red lights at me. I'd forgotten to turn my car's headlights on. He was kind and understanding—especially after checking my records in which he found no infractions or traffic tickets in the previous five years. He did not give me a ticket.

I continued driving home—and despite having had no food since breakfast, I wasn't hungry. I kept thinking about the almost two decades of yogic studies, hundreds of thousands of dollars spent in studies, seminars, courses, certifications, travels to India and around the country to learn from some of the greatest teachers.

Fortunately, in 2007, I came across some YouTube videos by Dr. Pillai—who later became my teacher and meditation guru.

He was *Wayne W. Dyer*'s guru, too, although I wasn't aware of it. If you don't know Wayne W. Dyer—he is one of my favorite authors of best-selling self-help and spiritual books. As it turned out, some of his books were dedicated to Dr. Pillai and his teachings.

And as good fortune would have it, within a few years my life began to blossom thanks to my studies with Dr. Pillai. I felt more fulfilled in my work and studies after I embraced his teachings. I was transformed into a better version of me. Later, I even began working for Pillai Center—Dr. Pillai's own organization of mind science. He taught according to the tradition of the Siddha yogis and masters of South India. This was the same lineage that I loved since I read *Autobiography of a Yogi* 20 years earlier.

In 2016, Dr. Pillai empowered me to become a *Pillai Center Teacher.* This was a great honor for me after so many years of spiritual yet unfulfilling work. I finally felt that my dream of helping others evolve and reach lasting happiness was coming true. And it has been very rewarding ever since!

Moral Victory

As for the health club—they're still offering the same *restorative yoga class* that I designed years ago. It turned out that I had quit too soon—and people had begun to acknowledge that they needed to slow down to avoid stress and injury from improper yoga practice.

Real Life

On the infamous September 11, 2001, after watching the news on TV, I was hyperventilating. The world was watching from all media outlets. Spectators were gripped by overwhelming fear—as it was later reported.

On TV, gut-wrenching news reports were delivered with spontaneous sounds of horror. My mind, too, was in a chaotic whirlwind and I couldn't move. I was at home alone, feeling like a deer in headlights as I stared at the horrific images in slow replay, capturing the same tragic attacks dismantling the Twin Towers.

Apocalyptic thoughts came to me: *Are we being attacked? Is this going to result in WWIII?*

After some time, I'd regained some control of my body-mind. I reached for the phone to call my mother in Italy. I felt pain in my stomach in hearing the recording saying that there was no phone connection.

I called my best friend in France. Again, the same sinister recording said that no international calls could be placed. I phoned my husband in his office and I finally relaxed as I heard his voice.

In a strange tone, he asked me, "Are you watching the news on TV?" I felt a bit reassured that in Chicago, where I lived, everything seemed normal.

Yet life had already changed for everyone on this planet. Sympathy and condolences for the victims' families and support for the American people were already pouring in from the rest of the world.

I couldn't stop my hands from shaking.

Then I remembered the yogic saying: *"Where do you go when you have nowhere else to go? You go within."* I realized that my only option for regaining control of my mind and body was to sit and meditate.

The technique was simple and it worked even on that day. I became calm. I was flooded with compassion for the grieving, petrified millions in the U.S. and around the world. In fact, I felt more love for humanity than I'd ever felt before. Moreover, fear vanished.

In my meditation, I saw scores of frightened Iraqi people, in deep grief from being bombed. I felt their pain as if it were my pain.

At the end of my meditation, I wondered about the meaning of that vision: *Why Iraq?* Every political commentary on TV talked about a possible war with Afghanistan. It took me almost two years to realize the truth of that vision, as the U.S. prepared to go to war with Iraq.

Transformation is Key to Experience Positive Change

The hours between 3 a.m. to 5 a.m. are known as *Brahma Muhurta—* or the time of the Creator God.

According to the yogis and sages of India—this is a time when your mind is most alert. Even 5 minutes of meditation during this time will increase your intuition, give you peace and bring creative solutions to your problems.

Meditation

- Set your alarm for 4:30 a.m.
- Set a timer for 15 minutes.
- Sit comfortably and close your eyes.
- Put your attention on your breath and nostrils.
- Gently, keep your attention on the breath and nostrils even when thoughts appear.

- Do not wrestle with the mind. If thoughts persist, accept them but go back to the nostrils each time.
- Eventually, the mind will calm down and you'll feel refreshed and energized.
- At the end of your meditation, you can go back to sleep.

Then notice how your day goes. You may find that you can conceive new ideas, and your activities go more smoothly. You may even receive the miracle you've been hoping for.

The usual hero adventure begins with someone from whom something has been taken, or who feels there's something lacking in the normal experiences available or permitted to members of his society.

—JOSEPH CAMPBELL

Because of the eighth house experiences, we usually feel that we've completely lost control over what we want from life. Yet it's from now on that you're given an opportunity to be a hero in your life and test your wings, like a human angel—in fact, this is also the house of metaphysics.

Even the darkest night will end, and the Sun will rise again.

—RUMI

NINTH SPIRITUAL LAW
Your Good Fortune

When you connect with higher sources of knowledge and inspiration, you find your higher Self. Then, miracles become your everyday reality.

9TH HOUSE

Trust, Higher Perspective, Wisdom, Law, Travel, Good Luck, Higher Education

---

One looks back with appreciation to the brilliant teachers, but with gratitude to those who touched our human feelings.

—CARL JUNG

Affirmation

The cosmos and benevolent celestial beings are my teachers. They guide me even in my sleep. The universe wants me to evolve and succeed.

Planetary Ruler of the 9th House

The planet of the 9th house is Jupiter.

JUPITER

- Positivity
- Expansion
- Space
- Wealth
- Children
- Faith
- Trust in the Divine
- Ethics
- Law
- Higher Studies
- Optimism

Jupiter is the planet that rules the ninth house. Jupiter expands everything it comes in touch with, including your faith. Thus, it increases trust in yourself, God, others, and can bring you wealth, optimism and a higher vision.

In fact, Jupiter gives you a higher perspective on yourself, your religious beliefs, and brings higher—the prerequisite for your awakening to your spiritual nature. Then, you tap into a field of infinite possibilities and you are more likely to fulfill your dreams.

The person who is always involved in good deeds experiences never-ending divine happiness.

—RIG VEDA

The ninth house is also connected to law studies and foreign travels, and good luck. Plus, according to the Vedas and the classics of Vedic astrology, dharma (or righteousness) and good fortune are connected.

Good luck can also come in the form of a Guru's blessings, positivity, past good deeds and help from your father. And your teachers can be heavenly messengers that help you evolve by showing you the right path. These human angels can also grant you guidance when you need to achieve your goals and increase your wealth.

Additionally, the ninth house indicates your greatest guides and teachers that help you uncover your spiritual self. This house or level of consciousness is also connected to your higher education, which contributes to your higher good and abundance.

Usually, the greater your knowledge, the more positive the results are for your work, income, relationships, and lifestyle. Yet the higher you search for your inspiration and knowledge, the more you'll find the Divine and satisfy all your material needs through faith and trust in a benevolent Source.

Meeting my Teachers

I remember the day I met one of my most influential teachers, Dr. Deepak Chopra. He was already well known and I'd loved reading all his spiritual books.

During that first lecture in upstate New York, I felt a strange expansion of my mind. I realized the meaning of the ancient teachings of the yogis and I felt infinite. I then realized that I could do anything and no limitation was insurmountable. I clearly felt my purposeful journey on this planet and I saw the endless weaving of events that had led to my spiritual studies, on that very day. My incredibly hard work and long, passionate studies of the Vedic arts and sciences finally made sense.

A few months later, I began studying at the Chopra Center in Carlsbad, California. For years, I'd been learning *Ayurveda* and its healing techniques, and I'd just received my yoga and Reiki master certifications. So I was a spiritual teacher—yet doubts would often pop up and I wasn't sure how to proceed in my career.

It was incredibly heartening to receive the teachings of Deepak and Dr. David Simon, two amazingly skilled medical doctors, who had made the shift to teach Ayurveda. There is so much respect for the whole individual in Ayurveda and its remedies.

On the morning of the first lecture at La Jolla, I dressed up knowing that something significant would happen that day. So I took special care to wear nice clothes. I wore an Italian knit, sleeveless turtleneck with black yoga pants. I also bought a bright-red pashmina shawl at the local store on campus to wrap myself against the cool December breeze.

I was looking forward to having Dr. Chopra sign my copy of "Perfect Health," one of his bestsellers. So during a short break in the lecture, I waited in line with about ten people in front of me to have the book signed. Then, realizing that the lecture would soon restart, I gave up and turned around to walk back to my seat.

I was surprised when someone tapped my arm, as I didn't know anyone there. When I turned, I saw Deepak Chopra standing in front of me smiling, and offering to sign my book. To me, this gesture seemed like a gift from the universe. His kindness and depth of knowledge helped me to believe in myself and my dream of becoming an inspirational, spiritual teacher.

Being in the presence of great teachers, and receiving their sincere support can make you feel that you, too, can successfully follow in their footsteps.

That afternoon, Deepak returned and began by telling us a story of synchronicity.

Real Life

When Deepak was a boy, his mother woke up one morning and announced that she absolutely needed to buy a new sari. She ignored her family members' comments that she already owned many lovely ones.

She was unmovable, insisting that she needed a beautiful, new dress because she was going to see Prime Minister Nehru during his visit to their town, Jabalpur.

Her family members argued that Nehru wouldn't even be able to see her because certainly, thousands of people would show up for the political parade.

Deepak's mother was unconvinced by these objections and insisted that for sure Nehru would notice her. For this, she had made the resolve that she would look her best. She was firm on this point.

So she bought a new silk sari. On the day of the parade, she wore her new dress and stood confidently in the front line of a very large crowd.

Then, the motorcade accompanying Nehru and other dignitaries made its way through the roads of Jabalpur, along the crowded sidewalks.

Here is the story as Deepak told it:

"She actually did catch Nehru's eye! He paused for a second, and then reached for the single red rose he always wore in his lapel. He tossed it to her. Even in all the tumult, my mother caught it."

Deepak's story was full of remarkable synchronicities and in my mind, I revisited similar episodes in my life, which were nothing short of miraculous. Since my childhood, I had honored my intuition—considering it a divine gift that protects us and helps us evolve.

Clearly, Deepak's mother, too, had attributed great importance to her own intuition. I then realized that life was a mysterious series of events conspiring to fulfill our destiny. And I marveled at the perfection of God's creation and the universe.

Sitting in the auditorium's front row and lost in these thoughts, I noticed that Deepak had stepped on the podium. I watched him as he picked a red rose from the bouquet in a vase on the table. He then came down, walked towards me and handed me that rose.

I could feel my back tingle with everyone's eyes watching me. I felt my face become warm. Yet for some strange reason, I wasn't too surprised. It was as if I had expected this gesture all along.

Intuition and Higher Teachings

Once the highest intelligence dawns on you, then everything is so easy. There is no labor at all.

—DR PILLAI

There are now plenty of scientific studies that prove the multiple benefits of meditation. According to both yoga science and neuroscience, meditation calms the nervous system, reduces stress, and activates parts of the brain connected with higher intelligence.

I've experienced that regular meditation can increase your intuition, reduce fear and remove mental and physical blockages. And with a strong intuition, you will naturally be attracted to what is truly good for you and your soul.

In fact, meditation is not just a technique for calming the mind and relaxing the body—as relaxation is just one of the byproducts of your meditative practice. With proper guidance, you can activate unused areas of the brain connected with supernormal powers of thought manifestation and omniscience.

Moreover, difficult personality traits that could be blocking your success—like anger, excessive focus on the self, or resentment—can heal spontaneously during meditation and thanks to increased awareness.

And when you remove subconscious blockages, you will acquire higher self-esteem. Without any makeovers, you will feel more attractive and might meet kinder, more loving people—thanks to the principle of *like attracts like*. You will become more loving, and others will respond in kind.

Real life

How I Met Dr. Pillai, My Most Important Teacher

I was living in South India in 2007, and it was still the rainy season when I began watching Dr. Pillai's YouTube videos on my computer. Everywhere in India, jubilant crowds were celebrating *Ganesha Chaturthi*, the birthday of the elephant-headed God. I had emailed one of my dear yoga teachers to wish her a Happy Chaturthi. And in her reply, she had told me about Dr. Pillai.

Looking at his videos, I recognized him, I had been looking for a teacher like him for decades. In fact, despite my 20 plus years of spiritual studies, no other teaching has sounded so close to my spiritual needs and hopes.

Now I believe that Ganesha was instrumental in removing the obstacles to my spiritual growth—something this God is famous for.

When I returned to the U.S. a few months later, I found out that Dr. Pillai was coming to New York City. I immediately signed up for his one-day seminar. I had already followed Amma and Sri Sri Ravi Shankar, yet I never felt they were my gurus. Of course, I was very grateful to them and loved their teachings. But something in me was unfulfilled.

When I met *Sri Dattatreya Siva Baba*—Dr. Pillai's spiritual name in the mid-2000s—I walked into the conference room of a Manhattan hotel that morning with no particular expectation.

Soon after he entered the room and I put my eyes on his slight figure, my spinal column began vibrating. These vibrations continued for the entire time I was in his presence. I remember that I was infused with a deep state of contentment. All my worries had vanished, my concerns forgotten. I did not analyze what I was experiencing—the way I usually did with other teachers. I simply sat there and loved infusing my mind and soul with his words.

I remember that even after I left, I still felt bliss and my spinal column kept vibrating for hours as I drove home. Ever since, I've simply considered him my Guru, and have never missed another of his teachings, seminars, programs or videos.

I became committed without even having to make the decision—because every word he said and every teaching or technique he gave us was instantly recognized by my soul as something I already knew, as if I were simply remembering.

Most of who we are is not accessible to the conscious mind under normal circumstances.

—DR. MITCHELL GIBSON

Meditation

Dr. Pillai's Karma Busting Technique

- Set a timer for 5 minutes.
- Sit in a quiet place and close your eyes.
- Visualize the Sun entering your *heart chakra* in the center of your chest.
- Now visualize the Moon entering and merging with the Sun in your heart center.
- Continue this visualization until the bell rings.

- Then relax.
- Slowly open your eyes.

Practice this meditation often. Your ordinary thoughts blocking manifestations will be dissolved and your manifestations will speed up.

If you can dream it, you can do it.

—WALT DISNEY

Real Life

In a night full of pain and darkness, be a candle spreading light until dawn.

—RUMI

Have you ever had a personal experience of the so-called *dark night of the soul?* This spiritual experience can be painful, yet it is not considered a negative event. In fact, at this time you could hear your soul whisper:

"I need a better life. I am meant for more than just hardship and delays to my goals. I want to know God. I want happiness."

One night about 15 years ago, I went to bed in a deep state of grief. I felt wide awake as my thoughts wouldn't allow me to sleep. I felt that my life had been a waste of time: so many trials and difficulties, hard work and few rewards. I also felt misunderstood by my female friends—who weren't particularly interested in my spiritual path, and would rather enjoy their wealth, vacations, and family lives.

At that time, I was oppressed by worries about my future and the job I'd just quit. I felt overall hopelessness.

After crying inconsolably for over an hour, I saw a light in my mind's eye. A bit startled, I opened my eyes and looked at the clock on my nightstand: it was 2:30 a.m. When I closed my eyes again, the light was still there and in it was a monk wearing a brown hood over his head.

His facial expression exuded pure love and great compassion. He told me gently, "All your problems will be solved." I was surprised, but not scared, as his words felt completely true. I somehow *knew* that he'd told me the truth. I took a deep breath of relief that made my heart and chest expand, feeling as light as a feather. All my fears and worries vanished. In their place came a feeling of safety and being taken care of by the Divine. Soon I fell into a refreshing sleep.

Within a few weeks, literally, all my problems around money, work and home-related issues were solved. I also decided to follow my dream: a month later, I enrolled in a yoga teacher's certification program. From this particular step came wonderful changes and I never looked back.

Moreover, now I know that after the dark night of the soul comes a radiant dawn—an effulgent light and unexpected solutions. We are constantly being guided and watched over by benevolent light forces that want to help us succeed in our goals, and guide us to spiritual evolution.

You're never truly alone—and even in your darkest moments, celestial beings are ready to intervene on your behalf to solve your problems.

You Are a Co-Creator with God and the Universe

According to the yogic tradition, the Guru is the representative of God on the earth plane, because God cannot come to this earth plane directly.

—DR. PILLAI

We must learn to guard our thoughts or we'll be controlled by the mind's negative tendencies: fear, self-doubt, skepticism in the existence of a Higher Power, negative expectations, lack of compassion for others' suffering, hatred, and more. Dr. Pillai says that the mind is 99 percent negative and these thoughts come from the neocortex.

We have mistakenly called the midbrain and cerebellum the *primitive brain.* Together they actually form the so-called *divine brain,* where all the hidden supernormal powers reside.

You have hidden powers: for example, even by simply observing your thinking patterns (without believing every thought), your life can change for the better.

You'll realize that many of your usual statements are based on beliefs you no longer hold about yourself and your life. In fact, you'll notice that many thoughts are similar to your parents' thoughts, your siblings' thoughts, your peers' thoughts—and worse, your enemies' thoughts.

Even when you choose a new teacher, it's a good idea to make sure that this person truly reflects your highest values, beliefs and he or she *walks the talk.*

Trust yourself and trust in your Self: this is the message of Jupiter whose Sanskrit name *is Guru—the dispeller of darkness.*

Your observations and impressions are creating your reality every moment. Did you know that an observer can change even cells in a laboratory through the power of his or her consciousness? According to quantum physics, we can even change the nature of particles through our predictions—a process called by the yogis the *observer's reality.*

The Tamil Siddhas and the yogis were able to see the different spaces, innumerable spaces beyond the tridimensional space, which Einstein talked about, as well as the fourth dimension of time.

—DR. PILLAI

The Power of Belief

You are here to enable the divine purpose of the universe to unfold. That is how important you are!

—ECKHART TOLLE

We must avoid believing a negative identity about ourselves. Statements such as, "I'm too old; I'm too small; I'm powerless" are untrue beliefs. Holding positive thoughts about yourself and others can transform your life, fulfill your wishes, increase your wealth and enhance your life experiences.

For example, there have been famous people—geniuses in their fields, who had been grossly underestimated by their teachers, peers and families. But these well-known individuals kept faith in themselves and later became world renowned for what they did or discovered. You'll recognize their names—Albert Einstein, Michael Jordan, Steve Jobs, to mention just a few.

The yogis are examples of utter positivity and their amazing feats stem from their pure consciousness, which allows them to identify themselves with God.

In fact, they regularly affirm that they are God—and have developed supernormal powers that prove their omniscience, omnipotence, and omnipresence.

It's very important to think beyond yourself. When you begin to have that type of thought, your consciousness expands to make your thinking universal.

—DR. PILLAI

Dr. Pillai says that the *observer reality* is the only reality. What you expect you'll get. This confirms spiritual teachings from the spiritual masters: *To be successful, think positively, see good, do good, expect good.*

Only then, can we gain more control over our negative mindset—or karma—and avoid the destructive effects of negative thought forms.

By remaining in a happy state of mind, you'll experience miracles. I have experimented with these teachings many times and I found them to be true.

May the blessings of universal Soma flow into our lives, enriching us with cosmic vitality, unveiling a deeper perception, the intuitive eye and a gentle concern for all. May there be love, light and bliss throughout our lives.

—SHAMBHAVI CHOPRA

The goal for you is to remain open to miracles and trust that your intention is a powerful form of energy. Keep in mind that you're meant to experience positive results and wish fulfillment. It's your destiny.

Meditation

Choose an archetype—a Goddess or God whose name and qualities resonate with you. If you're not familiar with any of them, do a quick online search and trust your intuition. There's a good reason why a name came to you, and there isn't such a thing as coincidence. Trust this synchronicity.

Below are some choices.

Female Celestial Archetypes

- Lakshmi
- Parvati
- Lalitha Tripura Sundari
- Saraswati
- Tara
- Kuan Yin
- Isis

Male Celestial Archetypes

- Shiva
- Vishnu
- Brahma
- Ra
- Zeus
- Apollo

For a few weeks experiment with pretending that you own the qualities of the chosen archetype. You will experience an expansion of consciousness. And you may even receive a miracle—which is none other than a sudden and positive event we have no explanation for.

Higher intelligence resides with the archetypes, which live in the unconscious.

—DR. PILLAI

Meditation

- Sit in a quiet place and close your eyes.
- Mentally recite the sound *Om* (the universal sound of creation).
- Affirm: I am an infinite being of light and power. I am one with my Source.
- Continue to chant *Om*.
- Now, visualize yourself as a being made of light.
- Mentally send your love to all beings on this planet. Include yourself among the recipients of your immense love and respect.
- Relax and open your eyes.

Do not wait until tomorrow to meditate. Do not wait until tomorrow to be good. Be good now. Be calm now. It will be the turning point of your life.

—PARAMAHANSA YOGANANDA

I have nothing to add because the perfection is already there. All I must do is remove the unnecessary pieces.

—MICHELANGELO

TENTH SPIRITUAL LAW
Your Career and Success

When you find your unique path and ideal career, you will easily be successful and use your hidden talents. You will then fulfill an important reason for your birth, as your karma, duty, career, and success are all interconnected.

10TH HOUSE

Career, Public Life, Finacial Goals, Recognition, Success, Business, Maturity

---

The only way to do great work is to love what you do. If you haven't found it yet, keep looking. Don't settle.

—STEVE JOBS

Affirmation

I love what I do for a living. I fulfill my destiny with my talents. Every day I discover my hidden gifts and use them, so my work and life become more enjoyable and meaningful. My reputation is sterling and my career thrives. I always carry out my duties with joy.

Planetary Ruler of the 10th House

The planets of the 10th house are the Sun, Jupiter, Saturn, and Mercury.

SUN

- Self-respect
- Success
- Energy
- Higher status
- Government
- Wealth

JUPITER

- Inspiration
- Wealth
- Faith
- Optimism
- Higher principles

- Higher education
- Expansion

MERCURY

- Speech
- Business
- Writing
- Communication
- Analysis

SATURN

- Commitment
- Perseverance
- Duty
- Rules
- Longevity

Just as the Sun is the central light of our solar system, it is also the source of our inner Light.

—DR. PILLAI

The planets of the tenth house, *Sun, Jupiter, Mercury, and Saturn,* represent all the laws that lead to a satisfying career and lasting success.

To succeed, we often need higher knowledge, hard work, commitment, perseverance, faith, and trust in our capacities, respect towards the existing laws and rules of our society, compliance with governmental regulations, intelligence, skills and help from authority figures. In fact, this is also the house that shows your activities in society and how you appear in your public life.

Right Goal Setting is Right Goal Reaching

The tenth house represents your career and how you can become successful. Because your work and financial conditions are interrelated, as you set your career goals—you're simultaneously setting your financial goals.

It's important to say that from both the yogic and astrological perspectives, being specific when you set your goals is paramount.

Apparently, this is also the opinion of researchers. A study of Harvard students found that after graduation, those who were in the habit of writing their goals and a detailed plan were earning ten times as much as the remaining 97 percent of the students who didn't.

We create karma. Nothing takes place in your life unless you think a thought, either consciously, unconsciously or subconsciously.

—DR. PILLAI

Planetary Help

- According to Vedic astrology, the Sun is your soul, but also your physical vitality. Moreover, the Sun gives you success, recognition, and wealth. So your work is driven by your soul's need to express itself on the earth plane through the physical body.
- Mercury is the celestial body of business, cash money, your communication style, and the devices you use to speak and write: computer, smart phone, tablets, video cameras, etc. Mercury is the intelligence to understand what is needed in the moment to accomplish your goals and enjoy your time with others. Also, Mercury helps you gain in commerce, bringing you excellent communication skills and effective strategies to reach your financial goals.
- Jupiter supports you with ethics, a greater vision, brings you good fortune, a positive philosophy and outlook, all kinds of wealth and trust in yourself and the Divine to reach even your greatest goals. Additionally, Jupiter teaches you righteousness, and represents the highest wisdom—or the intelligence to see the bigger picture and how to benefit all.
- Saturn is the planet of maturity. When we are young, we risk failing in our goals for lack of experience. Saturn brings you the perseverance and maturity you need to work harder, postpone

gratification and secure future rewards. If you want be successful, Saturn can help you by keeping you focused, no matter
how difficult work becomes.

Do What You Love

What do you really love doing? Is it an activity in which you totally
forget yourself and time goes by without you even realizing it? For example, you might forget to eat. You might tell yourself: *It's incredible—3
hours have gone by and I wasn't aware of it.* Can you make a profession
out of this activity?

When you're completely content and work effortlessly for hours at a
time and with great results, you are more likely to succeed.

You can then trust yourself to become a success as you engage in
what you really adore doing. Also, no matter what you do, if you add
fun (Mercury), inspiration (Jupiter) and perseverance (Saturn), success
will be certain, because the synergy of positive creative forces can bring
about the fulfillment of your dreams.

Success is not a choice, but a requirement.

—DR. PILLAI

Does Your Career Rhyme with Fear?

The only source of knowledge is experience.

—ALBERT EINSTEIN

Have you ever felt at some point in your career that you had reached
a plateau of boredom and meaninglessness?

If you've been feeling enslaved by your job, perhaps your intuition
could help you find a better job through new ideas, fortunate synchronicities and wish manifestation. Synchronicity comes through meditation and attention. Look around for clues. More often than not, you will
experience being at the right place at the right time. Or you could meet

that one key person that can offer you a new opportunity, or just the kind of help you need. It has happened to me countless times—but first I had to make a decision to stay more alert to clues and synchronicities from the Divine or the universe. We live in a connected universe and nothing happens randomly.

Meditation

- As soon as you wake up in the morning, try to remember your dreams. Even if you cannot at first, continue to do so every day.

This simple exercise will help you remember your dreams, which are often packed with revelatory symbols and premonitions.

- Write down any synchronicities that you experience throughout the day. For example, if you had a dream about a bicycle and during the day you see the same bicycle, notice that. Usually we get several signals of future events.

When you become more comfortable with your intuition, you'll receive guidance at every step of the way. So choosing the right work for you will become easier, too.

No one can benefit from a fear-based belief that there aren't enough good jobs available. And beliefs are usually manifested.

By honoring your spiritual self, and following an ethical path that reflects your life purpose, you will master the power to create your perfect career.

And wherever we put our attention, that is what grows. So never think that life is hard and full of obstacles—yes this might be true at times—but you will benefit more from believing that you always find a perfect solution and something better is in store for you at all times.

Can you remember the last time an obstacle turned into a springboard to better opportunities? Your answer will show you the way to a better future and more meaningful work that rewards you with financial abundance.

Real Life

Why I Hated My "Ideal" Job
In my mid-30s, I landed what I called *my ideal job* within a cultured and multinational community. I helped organize cultural events, promoted inspiring events and truly enjoyed it.

We all got along great, shared interesting ideas, and collaborated in harmony. I held the highest rank after the director of cultural affairs, and our agency had jurisdiction in Chicago and 11 states in the Midwest. This may sound like a great responsibility, but to me it seemed like fun.

It was also fortunate that my top superior—the consul general of Italy—was happy with my work. On occasion, he even asked me to attend meetings with foreign diplomats in his place. Of course, I felt both honored and grateful for his trust.

After one such meeting, I reported to the consul general that the meeting had focused on the Chicago Film Festival, a big event with more than 50 participating countries.

Change of Pace

The former director of culture affairs, a man in his sixties with the unfortunate habit of shouting orders at subordinates, had retired a few months before, and the new director had not yet been appointed. For this, everyone rejoiced.

Then about a year from the start of my work, finally a new female director was appointed. I remember the day she arrived from Italy.

We were all excited to meet her. She barely whispered a salutation. It seemed that a frown of displeasure had remained stuck on her mouth. We smiled nervously. Later, everyone confided that they'd felt really apprehensive because of her strange behavior.

It turned out that this was the new director's normal demeanor, which was a rare scene in our offices. In fact, whether it was the members of our community in need of cultural information about Italy, visiting celebrities or dignitaries, scholars and diplomats, everyone was usually cordial.

A few days later in the presence of the consul general and the ambassador visiting from Washington D.C., I realized that the female director was actually capable of smiling.

We often rolled our inner eyes in her presence, because, most annoyingly, she didn't give any feedback for our work. Sometimes she gave no sign of having heard what we said to her. She didn't thank us either. I began fidgeting in her presence.

Even her appearance exuded strictness: the dresses and skirts seemed a size too big for her small stature. The shoes had thick, short heels.

On her first day at work, she settled in her lovely office filled with Italian artwork. The designer lamps added modern appeal to a corner view of Michigan Avenue, the Chicago street filled with renowned architecture and upscale retailers.

She closed her door and never came out until the end of the day. She communicated with us through the phone. On the second day, she called me into her office and, without asking me to sit, came straight to the point.

Her severe tone immediately brought back memories of my long-gone school days. I noticed that by turning slightly sideways from her and avoiding looking into her eyes, I felt safer. Then I sat down.

"I understand that you're a member of the Women's Board of the Museum of Contemporary Art," she said. "I need you to write down the names of the director and the trustees." For a few moments I remained speechless, unhappy with her request.

I wondered how she'd found out my role at the museum, which was unrelated to my work for the Consulate General of Italy.

Of course, the names of the museum's board members were public—but her request seemed out of place. I also didn't feel comfortable refusing to help her. So I wrote the names on a block note that she'd pushed in front of me.

When I finished writing, I offered to accompany her in a tour and make the introductions. Her reply was stony silence. So I walked out of her office.

The next day, she called the museum's director and the chief curator, asked to meet them and went alone.

I felt equally annoyed and intimidated. I managed to resist these emotions, as I didn't want the quality of my work to suffer. But in the following days, while I was beginning to accept the new situation at work, I noticed some tightness in my chest throughout the day.

I knew my heart was very healthy and had recently tested in the top one percent for fitness and lung capacity. My routine of running, yoga, dance, and biking gave me enough energy to tackle a full-time job and caring for my family at home. But at the office I often shivered with cold and felt weak.

In the following days, I kept my focus on urgent projects and tried keeping a positive outlook, but the heavy heart sensation persisted.

One late afternoon, getting ready to go home, handbag in hand and coat on, I followed a sudden impulse. I dialed the office of a celebrity filmmaker in Italy. No one had been able to secure an English subtitled copy of the Italian movie for the upcoming film festival. I wanted to make one last effort.

The problem was the time zone: 5 p.m. Central meant midnight in Rome.

I thought: *I'll leave a voice mail for the director's assistant.* Others in my office had said that she was adamant: she couldn't provide a subtitled copy of the new film.

Power of Synchronicity

I heard the phone ringing on the other side. "*Hello,*" a male voice said. I quickly introduced myself—I had not expected someone to answer.

Though, I soon recognized the voice of the famous film director. It seemed strange that he'd answer his office phone at that late hour. He told me that he'd stopped by the office to get some documents.

"*We still need a subtitled copy of your movie for the Chicago Film Festival,*" I said. His voice sounded warm and friendly—and he quickly promised to send me the film by messenger the next day.

Bingo! I felt like dancing for this success. Two days later, I signed the slip that a courier brought into my office. I immediately informed the consul general and he congratulated me.

This outcome must have been the result of my daily meditation, as my intuition seemed stronger every day, and I noticed more and more positive coincidences.

Naturally, I wanted to share my victory with the director. I expected her to be ecstatic—and that maybe she would relax her demeanor a bit. But her response came as usual with a closed-lipped stare.

The next morning, she suddenly appeared in my office. "*I'm very upset with you!*" she said in a high-pitched tone. "*I can't find the receipt from the film's delivery!*"

I managed to apologize and mumbled that it must be in the film festival's file. Maybe her secretary had put it there. My subtler meaning was that one of the secretaries was supposed to file the receipt. She continued to argue with me that all receipts must be found in the right place.

This seemed to me like bureaucracy at its ugliest. Moreover, the overnight delivery had been paid by the movie director, and the receipt didn't seem to me as important as having the copy of the film—which I'd already sent to the festival's organizers. These were my thoughts as I drove home.

At home, I sat motionlessly on my burgundy sofa—my favorite meditation spot. I just stared through the window in front of me with no desire to move, cook, eat, or talk to my sweet children. I felt spent.

Was I overreacting? I wasn't happy and I trusted that feeling! When the nanny left, I shook my body and rolled my shoulders—as I did sometimes after sitting for long hours. Then I regained some energy, and I cooked dinner.

The next morning, I didn't want to go work. My body did not want to leave the bed. But I thought that self-discipline would probably solve my problem.

So at 5 a.m., I practiced my usual yoga and meditation, wrote in my journal, and at 7 a.m. I skipped morning coffee, as I felt my chest become tight at the thought of the office.

After helping my children get ready for school, I drove to the gym and took a vigorous spinning class.

I resisted the desire to call in sick, but after the shower, I wore the suit I'd carried in a garment bag and drove to the office.

After leaving my car with the attendant in the building's garage, I stepped into my office. Then I saw her, my boss. She was accompanied by a group of dignitaries. She neither replied to my salutation and nor introduced me.

About an hour later, she stormed into my office. "Never," she shouted, "do such a thing again!" She waved a large checkbook that I'd left on my desk the day before, forgetting to put it back in my desk drawer. I sincerely apologized. Clearly, the tension at work was starting to get to me—I had never left the checkbook out. It was my responsibility to make sure it was locked in a safe.

At lunchtime, I had a stomach ache. Again, I noticed the tight feeling in my chest. I felt tears coming: Am I being unappreciated for my work and as a person?

I skipped lunch in my favorite restaurant. I strolled down Michigan Avenue. Despite my new English raincoat and the Italian pumps, I felt like a homeless woman. I kept mulling over the past two months since the arrival of the new director.

Seeking Grace

Then the crystal-clear truth hit me—my work life had turned into a hell of powerlessness and humiliation. I resisted the tears and quickly made a decision.

Seconds after walking back and entering the director's office, I looked right into her eyes and said: "*I resign and I'm leaving today.*" Regrettably, my voice didn't sound as calm as I'd hoped. Nonetheless, I was proud of my courage.

"No, you can't!" my boss literally shouted. "You forget that you need to give a one-month advance notice."

I was silent for a few seconds then walked out. I entered a large office where the two secretaries sat at their computers. I tearfully confided what had just happened. One of them told me smiling: "You're so lucky, you haven't taken your 6-week vacation this year! You can leave today.

I literally hugged this girl who had instantly solved my problem. I quickly returned into the director's office, and told her the news! Now she was speechless. On my way out, I left her door open.

As I walked back to my office, I felt incredibly happy, the tightness in the chest had disappeared.

Thirty minutes later, I said goodbye to my nice coworkers, who told me they would miss me and that they wished they, too, could quit. Fortunately, after that day, we remained friends and stayed in touch for years.

As I walked by the director's office, I noticed that her door was still open. Then I heard her shout at someone on the phone: "She hasn't taken her vacation!" Clearly, she was talking about me. Her strident voice made me even happier for my regained freedom.

Fear of Change

As I was leaving my no-longer ideal job, thoughts began to dawn: *I don't want to leave my dear coworkers. And I love my office. I'll never see the pretty skyline behind my desk again.*

A small bronze bust of Victor Hugo—an antique gifted to me by a dear friend—looked so dignified on the desktop. I placed the statue in my tote bag. I liked beauty and design, and having my own office seemed like an obvious sign of success.

Fortunately, I realized that attachment was the dark forces' trick to keep us stuck in unhealthy situations.

I spent the following week in bed with the flu and a mysterious back pain, reading spiritual books, eating peanut *M&M's*—and breaking away from my usual diet of fresh, organic foods.

I worried that I'd never get another job—certainly not one with a six-week, fully paid vacation. I'd lost my nice, supportive team, and my office. Images of cubicles came up. Or worse, unemployment! Pessimism kept beating my mind.

The reactions from friends and family were the same—consternation and advice to reconsider. I felt let down and misunderstood by all.

But I didn't regret my decision. In fact, I also felt immense relief and a renewed sense of purpose. I wrote down my new goals.

New Resolutions That I Still Keep Today

After that unpleasant yet soul-freeing event, I vowed to work only with like-minded, cooperative, and noble individuals who value self-expression, want to make a difference while making a good living. I wanted to meet people with a great vision and not just a self-serving one.

And, this was non-negotiable, I wanted respect and support. Of course, I would offer the same to others.

Visualize It

I wanted more time for meditation, yoga, and my spiritual studies—and I wasn't willing to turn into a work slave.

Also, I made a resolution: until my children would reach college age, I would no longer work 36–40 hours a week, as I had. I wanted a part-time job.

More importantly, I wanted more time with my kids, and I was really unhappy about leaving them with nannies and babysitters.

I wrote it down: *Max 20–hour workweeks.* I soon manifested all the above goals—as I began working in public relations.

Success must be a joyous journey, a practice and discipline of expressing ourselves and pursuing our dreams.

—BRENDON BURCHARD

Insufficient Reasons for Staying Stuck in a Bad Job

We sometimes make excuses for remaining in difficult situations.

- I like my income.
- I like the car that my job pays for.
- I like the short commute.
- I like my coworkers.
- I'm afraid that I cannot get anything better.

Although the above are not invalid reasons, they usually don't reflect your great dreams. Wouldn't you rather do the following?

- Uncover your hidden genius.
- Leave your mark in the world.
- Express your creativity and help others.
- Be happy, and have time to travel or meditate.

Ask Yourself

- What kind of career do you *really* want?
- How do you want to be perceived in your society?
- What kind of activities would you be supporting with your wealth?
- What kind of work are you great at?
- How do you want to make a difference?
- How do you add value to others' lives?
- How do you want to express your talents?
- How do you want to inspire others?

Once you're certain about your authentic desires, then take action with that information in mind. Keep a log of even small victories towards realizing your vision and goals. This technique will increase your awareness and keep you more alert—so you will not act automatically according to the old mindset that brought you the job you hated.

The Power of Your Beliefs

I invite you to consider which beliefs might be negatively affecting your energy, finances, creativity, and income. Is there something that you need to let go of before you can reach the level of abundance and success you want?

Even if you cannot immediately let go of your unfulfilling job, can you find ways to make it more appealing?

After all, Rome was not built in a day—but when you allow yourself to find meaningful and satisfying work that makes you look forward to each day, you'll be more successful.

You can allow yourself to be happier, become more alert to the thoughts and beliefs you keep, and choose carefully what you host in your mind.

Once you make the decision and let go of any denial, you'll be able to find another job, or a service or new product to market and sell profitably.

I've seen this over and over again—when we change our thoughts and beliefs, our circumstances and other people around us also change. And when they stem from a commitment to our happiness and purpose, these changes are incredibly positive and bring us happiness.

Success in anything is through happiness.
—MAHARISHI MAHESH YOGI

.

ELEVENTH SPIRITUAL LAW
Fulfill Your Wishes

When you realize that you're never alone and that you belong to a cosmic group of souls spanning the past, present and future, you experience amazing synchronicities. The fulfillment of your ambitions is being designed by the cosmos. And your connections, networking and friends will help you achieve greater success, abundance and prosperity.

11TH HOUSE

Ethics, Communication, Networking, Technology, Speech, Writing

---

We have to look at how important our thoughts are and how they structure our life. 'I don't have a job.' If you keep saying that, it will keep happening.

—DR. PILLAI

Affirmation

At all times the universe is planning the fulfillment of my deepest desires. My friends and acquaintances support me, and I find myself in the right place at the right time. My wealth comes to me easily from multiple sources, and I realize all my ambitions.

Planetary Ruler of the 11th House

The planets of the 11th house are Jupiter and Mercury.

JUPITER

One of the planets that best represents this house is the expansive, inspirational, and generous Jupiter.

Jupiter is the energy of "more" and a planetary representative of highest intelligence, wisdom, all kinds of wealth and space, considered the most evolved element.

As a natural ruler of the eleventh house, the largest planet in our solar system points to the higher path of ethics, so we can reach the highest pinnacles of knowledge and devotion to a higher Source. Moreover, Jupiter brings good fortune.

MERCURY

Also, curious Mercury holds the flag of the eleventh house, bringing lively, fast energy for communication, technology, business, speech, and writing to acquire cash money, and connect to others in our global communities.

We all want to live a joyful life, in which ambitions and wishes are fulfilled. Yet as social beings, we often need other people who can help us live a satisfying life of love, success, and happiness.

In fact, it is fundamentally human to desire happiness and gains from one's work. Even those few who choose asceticism hold a burning desire for spiritual enlightenment.

The eleventh house is the place in a horoscope highlighting your great ambitions and desires. This house speaks of possible wealth gain and the desire to leave one's mark in the world. In this house, you connect with others to receive and give support, lasting friendship, and material gains through networking.

Meditation

Shreem is a cosmic sound heard by the yogis in meditation. They realized that Shreem was made of powerful sound waves that could change negative, limiting thoughts of poverty into a strongly abundant consciousness. This transformation of the brain and consciousness turned mediocrity and dissatisfaction into wealth and joy.

- Set a timer for 30 minutes.
- Sit in a quiet place. You can also practice this at your desk—use a headset and begin.
- Gently close your eyes.
- Put your attention on your nostrils.
- Every time a thought comes, gently return to putting your attention to your nostrils.
- Take some time to relax your body and mind with this technique.
- Then with your eyes still closed, mentally or aloud recite the sound Shreem.
- Keep repeating the sound until you hear the timer ring.
- Then, relax. Keep your eyes closed for a few more seconds. Then, slowly open your eyes.
- Repeat this meditation as often as you like.

You will gradually notice your thoughts shift and you will begin to embrace higher and higher levels of abundance in your life.

Meditation can enrich every aspect of your life. Most people teach that to be spiritual means to be materially poor. But God is not poor—God has everything.

—DR. PILLAI

The Lotus Is the Archetypal Symbol of Lakshmi and Wealth

The lotus flower carries the energy and blessings of a beautiful archetype of wealth, Goddess Lakshmi. She is said to resemble the sublime beauty of this flower.

There are many testimonials that talk of the amazing miracles brought by Goddess Lakshmi. Try Googling her and immerse yourself in the miraculous stream of Lakshmi's interventions.

Goddess Lakshmi's boons include better goals, a great new job, a successful career, a bigger paycheck, beautiful cars and homes, lovely jewelry, luxurious vacations, and pure thoughts leading to spiritual evolution, joy and bliss.

The Goddess can clear all your fears, doubts, insecurities.

—DR. PILLAI

Moreover, Lakshmi is said to bestow 16 types of wealth!

- Fame
- Higher knowledge
- Superior strength
- Victory over enemies or competitors
- Beautiful and healthy offspring
- Happiness
- Higher intelligence
- Bliss

- Incredible beauty
- Gold and gemstones
- Abundant, delicious food
- A higher life purpose
- Pure thoughts
- Enlightenment through meditation and right conduct
- Perfect health
- Longevity

Her signature sound or mantra is *Shreem*. You can invoke her with this sound and ignite her energy to bring beauty and happiness into your life.

Vibrate at the Speed of Wealth

In the cosmos, all is vibration—this is the principle of string theory that closely resembles the teachings of the ancient seers, and yogis of India.

Mantras—or the traditional Vedic sounds that change the brain through their frequencies—can help you think powerful thoughts for success and wealth. Your brain will literally, vibrate differently.

Shreem is the sound of life. The sound of the soul that will persist forever. It is not the breath, it is the soul itself.

—DR. PILLAI

Real Life

"I hate my life—I have no friends," cried my 11-year-old son sitting on the indoor stairs at home, head in his palms and tears rolling down his cheeks.

He had just begun his new school year as a sixth grader. I sat next to him to comfort him: "I'm sure you'll soon make lots of new friends," I said. But he seemed inconsolable.

Yet within a few months, he had made friends with a large group of boys and girls and developed a great passion for playing the drums.

In fact, he soon found that he had a natural talent for this musical instrument. As a result of his music, his popularity among his friends kept growing.

By the eighth grade, his musical talents had expanded, and he even formed a small band with three friends.

Then his freshman year at New Trier, a leading public high school on the Chicago North Shore, brought him a new opportunity.

He and the other boys in his band were selected to play in the school's annual music competition—becoming the first freshman band at New Trier to participate in the 'Battle of the Bands' competition.

My son was overjoyed—this was a big win happening just at the beginning of his school year, which went a long way to boost his self-confidence just as he entered high school.

Long forgotten were the years of his struggle in making friends—and his associations with other musicians had helped him fulfill one of his major wishes.

Let It Go Global

Nothing can stop an idea whose time has come—think of companies such as *Apple, Google, Facebook, Snapchat* or *Instagram.*

What is your unique idea? Write it down—find a network of like-minded friends who can help you implement it. Don't give up until you see its fruition. Meanwhile, meditate and be charitable—these two steps are the foundational tools for wish fulfillment according to the yogis.

Innovation is not limited to technology, of course. Some ideas can help us evolve to bring about the change we want in society—such as eco-friendly environments, organic farming, natural cleaning, eating locally after decades of long-distance produce, or cruelty-free beauty products, gentle on the environment as they are on your skin.

Adding meditation, more love, more compassion, more sharing can bring changes that both support and enhance your life.

True friendship, we know, can add meaning and support to our lives. The great yogi *Paramahansa Yogananda* believed that a good friend is a gift from God—a friend from a previous life that has returned to share with you many delightful moments.

The Most Life-Changing Idea

Could the global clock now be ticking in favor of spiritual ideas and pursuits? I passionately believe so. Collectively, we are now gaining awareness of esoteric knowledge that was once reserved for spiritual initiates, or small groups of enlightened yogis.

There are different ways of looking at poverty. Spirituality is the greatest richness that can happen to a human being. It's not against any other richness; it is simply against all kinds of poverty.

—*OSHO*

Formerly secret knowledge often surrounds power vortexes—places where your consciousness can shift effortlessly, and lead you to healing or wish fulfillment. India has hundreds of such transformative places—and I have visited many of them with Dr. Pillai.

It's also interesting to learn how science is catching up with yogic knowledge, proving countless prior claims by the ascetics and mystics of India. New discoveries in neuroscience are proving the human brain's hidden potential with the help of new technology. A 2017 Harvard study, for example, in which Dr. Pillai participated shows that some yogic sounds activate specific parts of the brain connected with higher learning, memory and intelligence.

Also, the yogis have long spoken about energy: the energetic subtle body, or energy transmission from a master to a student. This energy is said to bring about healing and transformation to the recipient. And meditation is now available to millions, through classes, programs, spiritual retreats, a guru or a personal spiritual coach.

Authentic Desires Manifest

An *authentic desire* is a wish that can completely transform your life and lead you to your purpose, spiritual evolution and can add more meaning to your life. While all wishes that don't harm others are valuable and can be pursued, some wish fulfillment brings you your highest good.

For example, the eleventh house energy of desire and ambition can help you raise the consciousness on this planet with the help of your networks. And, needless to say, the world really does need you and your unique qualities, desires, consciousness, and talents.

Additionally, your desires could include love, beauty, and wealth for yourself. Plus, charity, compassion and service to those who suffer. And spiritual enlightenment, if you're so inclined.

The impossible is often the untried.

—J. GOODWIN

Ask yourself: "What is my number one desire? Money, fame, success... [fill the blanks]." Find your number one need or great wish and with it "structure the rest of your life," as Dr. Pillai says. Let that desire guide everything you decide and do.

Achieve Your Greatest Ambitions

You have to be close to who you are, what you want, and how you want it. Also, the closer you put your product to the consumer and the more authentic you are, the longer you will last.

—DIANE VON FURSTENBERG

Consider the impact that connections can have in your life—say for example good friends that help each other fulfill desires and achieve goals. Think also, how making your work valuable and appealing to the masses or a certain sector of the public can take you from obscurity to fame.

While the above might not be your primary goals, the importance of being compassionate and caring about future generations is what makes ideas great and meaningful.

So take a few minutes to establish how your work can benefit others today, and in the long term. Will you make a difference and give it all you've got? Or will you hold back and get distracted by trivia or momentary needs?

Don't Believe in Struggle

The Divine or Universe is always trying to get your attention—a repetitive sequence of numbers appearing to you in different locations, a person you meet at the perfect time, as if by celestial intervention, a friend who offers help when you are about to give up. The above, and more mysterious signs, mean that your gain and profits don't require struggling and waiting.

Also, be willing to offer a helping hand and assist your friends in fulfilling their desires and the universe will reward you! Even simply listening with compassion and willingness to offer your expertise can make a world of difference. And the world loves a helpful soul.

I remind myself every morning: Nothing I say this day will teach me anything. So if I'm going to learn, I must do it by listening.
—LARRY KING

TWELFTH SPIRITUAL LAW
Sanctuary, Quietude, and Bliss

You're a light being. You are made of light particles. Your life becomes heaven on earth when you find bliss in yourself. That is the truth of your being.

12TH HOUSE

Meditation, Creativity, Intuition, Spiritual Practice, Liberation

---

When attention is redirected to the heart, a recognition and a soulful attunement occur. We find ourselves whole again—a wholeness that shines as peace, joy, wisdom and love. Life flows like a river of light.

—MOOJI

Affirmation

I am the beauty of the cosmos incarnated in a physical body. I'm made of pure light. My quiet time alone helps me create and manifest my cherished dreams. I'm totally fulfilled.

Planetary Ruler of the 12th House

The planets of the 12th house are Saturn and Ketu, the south lunar node, and Jupiter.

JUPITER

- Inspiration
- Wealth
- Faith
- Optimism
- Higher principles
- Higher education
- Expansion

SATURN

- Commitment
- Perseverance

- Duty
- Rules
- Longevity

KETU

- Letting go
- Spiritual life
- Enlightenment

Saturn brings delays and forces us to mature and acquire more wisdom in order to fulfill our duties and succeed.

Ketu is an invisible planet and lunar node that indicates letting go of our material attachments to focus on the long-lasting benefits of our spiritual practice.

The twelfth house is the place in a horoscope that indicates our subconscious mind, meditative states, and liberation from an excessive focus on the body, material attachments and sensual pleasures. Yet this place indicates the sublime beauty of nature that can be felt in the heart, or in our spiritual sight through meditation.

Spiritual poetry can uplift our mood when we suffer from a loss or loneliness. In reality, time alone is a most precious gift for renewal and spiritual enlightenment.

Then we become connected to our authentic self or divine nature. We are at one with all of life and the Divine.

From the twelfth house, enlightenment nudges us to let go of noise and excessive worldly engagements, so we can spend time alone, and connect with our silent higher Self.

Meditation can also take you into a deeper space, free from painful mind chatter. In this space of pure awareness, you come in touch with your intuition and your most authentic desires—those that truly make your life worth living.

The twelfth house also shows that your imagination has infinite creative powers.

Your intuition and vivid imagination are, in fact, divine tools for creation.

Have you ever desired something so badly—a relationship or a bigger paycheck, or a new home—that you found yourself working incredibly hard to attain it, but still didn't get what you wanted?

And perhaps you thought that you were taking a course of action to success, but then stayed in an unhappy or abusive relationship, or in a dead-end job.

Such negative experiences give our God-given intuition a bad name. It was not our intuition that led to such painful experiences, but rather repetitive thought patterns or karma. Unconscious patterns bring us impulses that resemble intuitions. So we make wrong decisions based on knowledge or understanding that doesn't come from the Self or the Divine.

Pure intuition comes from a peaceful state of mind and speaks in a gentle voice. Then the action you take is both righteous and beneficial to you in the long term. Your body too, is calm and comfortable when your intuition is at work because you're connecting with a very positive stream of consciousness.

After deep meditation for example, your imagination will spring from a higher place of knowingness. Then both your intuition and imagination will help you bring to life what you desire.

So hustle and bustle are not always necessary to experience the life we want. When you turn within, you'll give your material goals the *right* amount of space in your life—not more, not less.

You Are Light Particles

You will then take action at the appropriate time to experience your desired outcome. Ultimately, you'll know that you're more than your material goals—you are made of light particles, and your soul is eternal.

The Tamil Siddha yogis tell us that acquiring a body made of light is the ultimate state of human evolution.

I know that considering this idea from the standpoint of a hurried, busy day, packed schedule and tiring routines, makes it hard to believe that you can turn into light. Yet the yogis and other ascended masters such as Jesus have turned their physical bodies into light.

Tibetan monks have done that, too. They teach about attaining a *rainbow body* through meditation techniques.

Even Einstein believed in the light body. He said that not only is the light body possible, but that matter is just "*light stopped.*"

Moreover, quantum gravity tells us that reality doesn't even exist without our interactions. We are just vibrational interactions in space.

From the previous 11 houses, you have learned how to tackle everyday problems. Now it's time to turn within—where your maximum powers of creation and manifestation reside.

Intuitively we all know that we come from another world and that we did not originate on earth. Your dreams, daydreaming, and meditation are keys to discovering your divine origin, attaining wealth, and experiencing bliss.

So, we can understand why some people look for shortcuts and try to taste transcendence and bliss through artificial means like drugs or alcohol.

Unfortunately, such methods backfire and bring more unhappiness in the form of poor health, depression, or delusional states of consciousness, without any real spiritual or material progress. Whereas, the yogis teach that divine techniques for thought manifestation and wish fulfillment bring lasting happiness.

When you listen to your intuition and create through your imagination, you can achieve your goals faster than through logic.

So, don't feel guilty if you daydream. Allow that to happen—and use your deep, positive emotions to create a life you love. Learn to turn energy into matter and manifest your dreams.

The lessons of the twelfth house must be learned before we attain our supernormal power of thought manifestation.

Saturn is a great teacher, being the planet that teaches us to persevere, respect the rules of society, work hard and tend to our duties, and aspire to final liberation. Saturn delivers other lessons: Do your duty and work hard towards your goals, help others, be engaged in the world to serve and not just to enjoy.

Saturn also reminds us that we must assist underprivileged individuals—the disabled, homeless, elderly and especially those who don't have access to sufficient food, water, or clothing.

Jupiter embodies the highest intelligence, and liberation from ignorance, so we can acquire the spiritual knowledge about who we truly are. From this empowered state, we can acquire wealth in all forms—both material and spiritual wealth.

The kind of compassion taught by Jupiter is gently emotional and empathetic. You feel the pain of others. This planet of faith and optimism leads us on a path of higher knowledge and spiritual quest. Also,

Jupiter points to the emotional gentleness of solitude, nature, and lovely poetry filled with beauty and purity.

Ketu teaches that ultimately, you are not of this world—and it's good for you to take time off to let go of excessive attachments.

A balanced twelfth house does not lead to the belief that the world is "only illusion" or *maya*, and that we should renounce it, as some spiritual teachers believe.

Dr. Pillai says that the word maya—meaning the experience of life on earth—does not mean that all creation is a bad thing. Rather, maya must be enjoyed in order to live a balanced life on our planet. A *"200 percent life"* is more desirable, as it combines a 100 percent satisfying material life with a 100 percent fulfilling spiritual life.

For most people, letting go completely of the material reality in the hope to speed spiritual evolution can lead to health problems, excessive financial debts, and even hospitalization—all twelfth house themes.

A balanced approach to the twelfth house, instead, teaches us that we are God, and that we came here to acquire more knowledge, and feel compassion for those who suffer. So we must enjoy life, and do our work with love, charity, and contentment.

Thought Manifestation

I will speak what is right,
I will speak what is true,
May that protect me, may that protect the teacher.
May it protect me, may it protect the teacher.
Om Peace, Peace, Peace

—TAITTIRIYA UPANISHAD, I.I.I

Understanding the influence of the twelfth house can provide you with supernormal powers for manifestation. You'll learn to go within, meditate, and spend time alone in nature or your home. This will help you achieve the impossible. Also, according to the yogis and intuitive Rishis, solitude and silence are the traditional means to acquire omniscience.

Even Einstein explained that none of his theories and discoveries came from mathematical calculations. Rather, they all came from his imagination and were *revealed* to him.

Power of Compassion, the Highest Intelligence

Again, in "*How God Changes Your Brain,*" neuroscientists Newberg and Waldman tell us that meditation techniques trigger the brain, leading to neural activity that radically changes our perception of the world. They add that spiritual imagery leads to higher intelligence and compassion.

They conclude that, "the more we engage in spiritual practices, the more control we gain over our body, mind, and fate."

So through meditation, visualization, breathing techniques, chanting mantras, positive feelings, and thoughts we can literally change our lives.

The Power of Charity

Have you ever felt elated after a good deed, a food or money donation, or giving a helping hand to someone who was in need? Most of us have had moments like that. The well-being and bliss we feel when we give selflessly to others who are suffering stem from our soul showing us the way to perfect contentment and unity consciousness.

Dedication to a higher cause and filling our minds and hearts with inspired teachings that bring good into the world are necessary experiences to be the change we want to see and make a difference on this planet.

Intuition and omniscience bring you information that comes to you from within, without any research or study. They are gifts coming to you from powerful areas of the brain, primarily the pineal gland—or *third eye*.

Message from the Yogis

Yogis from the Tamil Siddha tradition, Dr. Pillai's lineage, believe that imagining a castle in the mind or '*building castles in the sky*' is no different from building a material castle on land.

Daydreaming happens in the *midbrain*, a part of the brain also known among ancient yogis as "the divine brain." A spiritual teacher or coach can guide you to experience the positive transformation and change to live the life of your dreams: a life of meaning and total fulfillment.

Your Dreams Matter

In dreams, your brain secretes DMT, which can lead you to lucid dreaming or out-of-body experiences.

The midbrain includes the pituitary and pineal glands and can create miracles. There is also a midbrain in the subtle body that is invisible to the eye, but well known to the yogis.

A miracle is thought-manifestation. A concrete way is using the midbrain. The yogis use this part of the brain exclusively and they don't have to wait. The problem is that the midbrain has been ignored by Western civilization.

—DR. PILLAI

Imagination Is Key to Your Happiness

Everything is an empty particle of consciousness, until we fill it with the will of imagination.

—DR. MITCHELL GIBSON

By surrendering to a Higher Power with the help of meditation and visualization, you can boost your brain's capacity to reach your goals and defuse the ego that says that what you want is impossible.

Meditation

- Sit down in a quiet place and close your eyes.
- Put your attention on your nostrils.
- Then say out loud (or mentally if it's not possible) what you want to accomplish: "I can have… I want." Fill the blanks with your wish.
- Repeat it 3 times.
- Now say out loud: "I can easily increase my…. (income, happiness, health, etc.)." Choose the one that applies to you. You can choose up to 3.
- Speak out loud and say that you're not scared of change.
- Say that you're willing to take the steps to experience what you want.

- Relax and when you're ready, open your eyes.
- Repeat this meditation every time you experience doubts about your capacity to manifest your dream.

Be Specific

I'm often asked: "How do you visualize something you want? Is there an easy way to do it?"

Yes, and even if you're not big on visualization, you can easily train yourself. For example: Can you imagine the house of your dreams?

- See its architecture.
- Dream it as fancy as you want it to be.
- Mentally, look at the colors of the walls.
- Touch the fabric of your new, overstuffed sofa.
- Sit on the velvety softness of that new chair.
- Look at the elegant shape of the coffee table.
- What green plants do you want to place in your lovely home?
- See and smell a bouquet of fresh flowers. What kind of flowers?
- Do you see multicolor, freshly cut roses as a centerpiece? Or soft colored peonies that evoke lovely images of spring and time in nature?

So, it's your home. Decorate it, change it, shape it. Sit and enjoy a cup of coffee or tea—or hot chocolate! It's your dream.

Cling to those lovely emotions and trust them. Your dream is meant to come true.

Again, feel the happiness for your manifestation! These steps are extremely helpful to get better at visualizing what you wish for, and you're giving your brain an experience of what you want, and what it really feels like.

When you can see your dream goal in your mind's eye in all its glory, it will be much easier for you to manifest it. And you will have fewer subconscious objections to your manifestation.

Use numerical figures if you want money. Decide ahead of time. That is precisely how you'll get what you want. Become acquainted with it and comfortable with it. Your intuition will take you right to the manifestation of your dream.

It is recommended that you don't jump ahead and state that you want millions or billions, if you're not already wealthy. The gap between your current finances and extreme wealth would be too big to fill in a short time, and it's likely that you couldn't conceive such a major change in lifestyle.

So, do it gradually: visualize a 5–10 times improvement in your condition. For example, if your income is $50,000 a year, visualize a $500,000 check. Then your subconscious mind will not sabotage your dream and you'll be able to conceive this new level of abundance. And after manifesting it, you can gradually increase the figures.

The intuitive mind is a sacred gift. The rational mind is a faithful servant. We have created a society that honors the servant and has forgotten the gift.

—ALBERT EINSTEIN

Real Life

On an eventful day on my children's school vacation, I went to work in the city as usual. My office was about an hour drive from home. Later, I received a frantic call from my kids' nanny.

Apparently, she had allowed my 10-year-old son to leave the house alone. "I'll be right back," he had said. He'd been gone for most of the day, and it was already late afternoon when she finally called me and confessed that my son was nowhere in sight.

After that news, I felt sudden chest pain and wondered whether I was about to get a heart attack. I immediately got in the car heading home to the Chicago north shore.

At home, I phoned all the mothers of my son's schoolmates, in vain. No one had seen Randy.

Just before I called the police, my son returned. He told me he'd taken a train to the city with a friend.

Together, two small boys had roamed alone in the big city of Chicago, well known for its high crime.

Finally, the tired boys had taken the train back home in the early evening. Just thinking what could have happened brought me to tears. I resisted a strong desire to fire the nanny on the spot. But I needed to go to work the next day, and that evening I certainly had no time to interview new women to care for the boys.

A few days later, again at the office, I received another call from the same nanny. She said that the children had been rough housing, running around in their socks.

This time she spoke calmly, as if nothing special had happened. To my question on the reason for call, she finally added, "Nick fell and broke his front tooth. He is bleeding." He was only 8, and his front teeth were his new, permanent teeth!

"How could you let them run in their socks?" That was all I could mumble. She remained silent. Again, I returned home speeding through traffic.

At home, I took care of Nick's lips and medicated the bloody cuts. On the phone, I made an appointment with his pediatric dentist for the next day.

Then I called the nanny into her bedroom, staring in disbelief as she casually began brushing her hair and talking about trivia. I had expected an apology or some sign of regret. I motionlessly looked her brush covered in loose hairs.

Something about her apparent indifference made me nauseated. I left the room while she went about her business.

I quickly returned and saw my hand tremble as I handed her a check for a full month's pay. My voice sounded angry: "Leave now, pack your things and go. We no longer need you." She neither pleaded nor showed any remorse.

That same night, I made a decision that changed my life forever: going forward I would return home around 3 p.m.—before my children came home from school. I longed to greet them at the door every day, and hug them, talk to them, give them snacks, check their homework, and engage in all other motherly activities. I wanted to nurture my children and didn't care about the money loss. I would gain so much more: happiness, peace and joy.

The next day, I stayed home and quit my job. Two weeks later I took a part-time position as a publicist in a public relations firm located just a 10-minute drive from my house.

My working hours, too, were delightfully short—10 a.m. to 3 p.m.—which allowed me to be home in time to open the door for my children every day after school. It was a new life, one that made us all much, much happier.

Of course, letting go of the nanny meant a lot more work for me. I had to pick up my children's clothes, put them in the washing machine, prepare their meals, drive the boys to their sports practices.

Yet after letting go of my prior lifestyle, I felt completely fulfilled. My lack of worry and guilt made me realize that those negative emotions had been draining my energy, and I now felt a lot stronger. My energy levels were higher and I never felt tired.

Of course, when we experience sudden change we feel that we're losing control. But in the bigger scheme of life, letting go is often necessary before we can experience the level of happiness and joy we want.

Love Yourself and Boost Your Energy

The yogis believe that in order to reach any goal—a successful career, lasting well-being, greater happiness, and bliss—you need to recharge your spiritual and mental batteries by connecting with your authentic Self.

In fact, we often identify ourselves with our 50–60 thoughts a minute and deep-seated fears. Instead, our higher Self is a reliable source of wisdom, intuitive knowledge and true power.

How do you connect with your higher Self? Through silence, meditation, alone time, perhaps in nature, and by noticing synchronicities—which are signposts that the soul uses to direct your attention from mundane reality to your inborn wisdom.

Also, when you practice meditation, you can connect with your Source, whether you call it God, Universe, Self or any other name. This is your way to growing your miracle-making abilities.

Secrets of the Yogis

I cannot overemphasize the importance of meditation to transform a noisy mind full of repetitive thought. In fact, like the yogis, you can find your supernormal powers in your brain.

These extraordinary capabilities can be discovered and activated through meditative practices that stop mind chatter and awaken the more powerful, intelligent brain—the midbrain, which is below the mushroom-shaped neocortex. Although we need the neocortex to function in this society, learn science, technology and math, the midbrain bypasses logic and can help you manifest your cherished goals.

The so-called third eye or pineal gland is part of the midbrain.

Midbrain Meditation

- Sit in a quiet place and close your eyes.
- Put your attention on your nostrils.
- Now focus on a point in the middle of your eyebrows, just above the nose.
- Now mentally move up to a point in the middle of the forehead.
- Keep your attention on this point.
- Visualize a bright, golden light on this point.
- Visualize the object you desire in this point.
- Then relax, and slowly open your eyes.

Repeat this meditation often, and even throughout the day, keep your awareness of this point in the middle of your forehead. Soon, you will notice that your intuition will increase. Better yet, you will be able to both conceive and manifest what you want.

What you visualize in your pineal gland, or third eye, will manifest.

The infrared in the midbrain can work like a remote control to get what you want, provided that you spend time tuning in to access your intuition. For the yogis, the midbrain includes the *third eye* or pineal gland.

Additionally, time alone does more than awakening your intuition and bringing you more accurate knowledge about yourself and the world. According to researchers, spending some time alone every day to care for your needs is essential to experience happier relationships.

Remember: when you meditate regularly, your capacity to visualize will grow and your intuition will awaken even more. You're already intuitive and you have probably experienced how it works. But it will grow even stronger.

Below are some of the amazing gifts that intuition can bring you.

- You'll be in the right place at the right time.
- You'll know whether you should send your resume to a certain company or choose another.
- You will know whether investing more money in your startup will be profitable.
- You'll choose a better partner or friend.
- Your intuition can even tell you when someone is lying to you.
- You'll be guided to select only trustworthy people for your daily interactions.

- You may take a walk in the park and end up meeting an acquaintance who offers to help you with your new project.

Detox from Bad Foods and Thoughts

Needless to say, if your body is starved for nutrients from eating wrong foods, your mind will be stressed too.

Do you remember the experiment at the Maharishi School of Management? The Maharishi School of Management, Iowa, made an experiment. Staff replaced the usual cafeteria food with warm, freshly prepared organic meals. Not only were the students healthier and in a better mood after switching to the new, healthier diet, but test scores were also higher and symptoms like ADD and depression disappeared.

Moreover, the yogis say that thinking too many thoughts is just as toxic as eating too much food. A calmer mind is focused, alert, creative and intuitive.

Intuitive knowledge is responsible for us to change the world. It's not through the rational process that we are going to find a solution.

—DR. PILLAI

I invite you to be gentle with yourself. Give yourself a short detox from excessive noise from media, city traffic or social life for at least a few hours a day.

Silence and time alone in nature are healing and blissful ways to recharge your batteries. When you're peaceful, you can become aware of what supports *prana*—or your divine breath known as *life force*.

Find your quiet place (even if it's just a corner of a room that you select) to find the *real you*. This could be your bedroom. It can be a house you rent for a month in the country or by a beach.

Ocean tides are the result of gravitational pull of the sun and the moon on the waters, as the earth spins on its axis. You have an ocean inside you that has the same rhythms—your circulation. Stay in sync with the cosmos.

—DEEPAK CHOPRA

Power of Poetry

The Vedas were written in verses, as poetry was considered a more effective, apt way to speak about our Source—and communicate with celestial beings.

And guess what: contemporary neuroscientists agree that poetry activates parts of the brain connected with more clarity and higher cognitive functions.

Mark Waldman, the author of *How God Changes Your Brain*, advices to write down your goals in a poetic form. They will be better grasped by the brain and you will achieve them.

Choose to immerse yourself in love, beauty, and light.

We have drunk the soma [or nectar of immortality]
We have become immortal
We have gone to the light
We have found the gods
What can hatred and the malice of a mortal do to us now?

—RIG VEDA

We Think and Manifest

Scientists tell us that neurons can be found throughout the body, and also in the heart. Not only does your heart feel, it actually thinks.

Meditation

Shift into Your Higher Mind

- Ask yourself what makes you truly happy.
- Close your eyes and put your attention on your heart.
- Let it speak to you.
- Accept what comes and thank your heart. If tears come don't suppress them.
- Make a powerful intention that today you'll choose only positive thoughts of love and gratitude.
- Relax.

- Slowly open your eyes.

Do this as often as you can—you'll feel refreshed and you'll increase awareness of your self-talk. This small shift in consciousness can change your life for the better.

Thought manifestation is the ultimate teaching, and everybody has the ability to do it.

—DR. PILLAI

Creative Visualization and One-Pointed Focus

Meditation allows you to get in touch with your true self, which is a field of infinite possibilities, infinite creativity, synchronicity, and power.

—DEEPAK CHOPRA M.D.

Meditation

Visualization
How will my life look 1 year from now?

- Sit in a quiet place.
- Close your eyes.
- Be as relaxed as possible.
- Put your attention on your nostrils.
- Now put your attention on your heart.
- Imagine that you are walking into a beautiful garden.
- See the plants and trees.
- Visualize the grass.
- See birds and butterflies.
- Look at the sky and its colors at sunrise.
- Blue color, rose color, pink color, yellow color, orange color.

- Now you see a small temple and you enter it.
- A bell is hanging from the ceiling. You pull the cord to ring the bell.
- You hear a pleasant crystalline sound from the bell.
- Visualize your favorite celestial being (Lakshmi, Vishnu, Shiva, Ganesha, Mother Mary, etc.).
- This celestial being is benevolent and wants to help you.
- He or She now speaks to you.
- As you listen, an image appears in your mind.
- Go deep into this beautiful vision.
- What do you see?
- If you like the image, make it larger until it is life size.
- If you see a beautiful beach (or mountaintop, office, home, etc.) make the beach bigger and see yourself on it.
- Visualize yourself smiling with pleasure.
- Feel a gentle breeze.
- Enjoy the happy emotions. Feel the joy.
- Let it go.
- Relax.
- Open your eyes.

How infinitely beautiful and awe-inspiring your life will be. You will gain insights into the poetic aspects of nature, including galaxies, other living beings, celestial bodies, and the light and love that pervade the entire cosmos.

Everything you can imagine is real.

—PABLO PICASSO

Your inborn greatness together with your desires for evolution, peace, and bliss will lead you to realize your divine nature.

You're amazing, awe-inspiring and all you need is to shine these inner qualities onto your outer life. Let your true, divine self, your true self reach the surface through love for yourself and others. When you are in a state of all-encompassing love, everything seems magical, easy and playful. Be you.

Stop acting so small. You are the universe in ecstatic motion.

—RUMI

EPILOGUE

We are light beings—light particles. We can either embrace our limited identifications as an aging body, a mind constantly filled with thoughts, a name that was given to us, a nationality connected with only one tiny area of Earth, or a fixed income. Or we can choose the truth of our infinite, divine nature.

You are made of light. It is both your birthright and the most important job in your life to remember your immense potential and beauty.

As a by-product of this awakening to your highest truth, your work will flow naturally, your creativity will soar, and your life will take on new meaning.

After these discoveries, many people have gone ahead and become millionaires, others have become enlightened and acquired supernormal powers. The spiritual masters have selflessly helped us discover our hidden gifts and uncover our immense potential.

Your evolution is contributing to a better and more evolved planet. You can share your story, be more loving towards yourself and others. Love is God. Enjoy your experience on earth. Remember that living in the body means being bathed in *maya* or the illusion that we're separate from other beings.

Yes, life can bring loss and sorrow, but the yogis and spiritual masters have left for us an enormous wealth of knowledge and techniques. We can and must be very happy. That is our inheritance. We can even perform miracles provided that we have faith—even *"the size of a mustard seed."*

Be happy, joyful, blissful—that's the path of the great masters.

If at first the idea is not absurd, then there will be no hope for it.

—ALBERT EINSTEIN

It's been a great joy and privilege to share my experiences with you. And I hope that this book will become your springboard to realizing your dreams and tapping into your infinite potential.

The universe is waiting for you to awaken to your super powers within, and for you to accept your rightful share of abundance, happiness and bliss.

With much love and all my best wishes for you to live a blissful life.

Life is bliss. There shouldn't be any moment of unhappiness.

—DR. PILLAI

ACKNOWLEDGMENTS

My gratitude and love go to the people who bring much joy and meaning into my life: my children Randy and Nick, and my husband Frank. Thanks for their loving patience with me as I skipped vacations, museum outings, birthday parties and more, just so I could write and study.

Deep thanks to my mother Ivana Arnaldi and my step-father Rocco Matera for the incredible inspiration and support. Growing up in Italy, I've had the incredible luck of meeting gifted individuals who have encouraged my writing. In my natal country, my mother a famous journalist and opinion maker, and my step-dad a multi-published philosopher, saw the best in me and supported my early stints at writing. This book wouldn't exist if they hadn't been there. I'm also grateful to the press and TV personalities who hired me as a journalist in my early 20s when I was still petrified to put my name 'out there'.

My love and thanks go also to Chris, Karen and Melissa Riback for their genuine and loving friendship.

My infinite thanks go to my incredible teachers and mentors, Dr. Pillai (Babaji), Deepak Chopra, Dr. David Simon, Amma (Shailaja Pillai), Valli Wells, Vijayalakshmi, Ruth Rashman, Hanuman Das, Sucharita, Gina Guerrieri—and others, too many to mention here.

Deep gratitude and love to my dear friends Stefano and Claudia Cacciaguerra Ranghieri, Patty Sternberg, Diana DeMeuse and more, who have insisted over the years that I write stories, articles and books, and encouraged me to keep going despite the challenges of writing in a foreign language.

Special thanks to Stephanie Callegari and Sandhyadipa Kar, my dear friends and soul sisters who share my lifetime love for Eastern spirituality, and who have supported me when I doubted myself and my path. I'm also grateful to my longtime friend Charles Bernardini for his support and help with my very first articles on American politics. Gratitude also to my friend and fellow Vedic astrologer Kristy Cohen for her support and appreciation of my writings and work.

And last but not least, deep thanks to my editor and publisher Alice Maldonado for her magical touch and apparent ease in editing and supporting the completion of *Bliss Lab*.

Finally, this book is both deeply personal and a carrier of my great hope that we all transcend everyday struggles to choose a life of ease, love and compassion for all beings, abundance, joy and bliss.

INDEX

www.ingramcontent.com/pod-product-compliance
Lightning Source LLC
Chambersburg PA
CBHW022124080426
42734CB00006B/238